Anne-Marie

...a Child of God

Psalm 102 v. 18:
"Let this be written for a future generation, that a
people not yet created may praise the Lord."

ISBN 978-0-9556758-0-5

Contents:

Foreword	5
Acknowledgements	6
Dedication	7
Preface	9
Early Days	11
Clark Clinic	37
Intensive Care	63
Munich	94
The Operation	129
Back to Base	150
A Short Life	169
Birmingham	193
Our Way Home	226
The Day of the Funeral	245
Life after Death	262
Into the Future	281
Afterword	294
Epilogue	296
Appendix	298
About the Author	310

Foreword

By Dr Brian Craig, Consultant Paediatric Cardiologist at the Royal Belfast Hospital for Sick Children

For almost 20 years I have had the responsibility of providing medical care for infants and children with congenital heart disease. During this time it has been a privilege to get to know many families and to have had the opportunity of sharing in their joys and also in their sorrows. I never cease to be amazed by the courage and fortitude shown by so many families in coping daily with a child who has a serious heart condition.

One such family is the McBride family from North Belfast. This book details the story of Anne-Marie, carefully and lovingly penned by a mother who selflessly shared in every aspect of Anne-Marie's short life. The gifted use of language imprints many lasting images within the mind's eye of the reader. The images are those of a child who, despite her frailty, had entered life fully, secure in the knowledge of a close and devoted family.

Although Anne-Marie's death is initially shocking and disturbing, the author's honesty, integrity and unshakeable faith in God compel the reader to consider Anne-Marie's life and death in the context of God's overall plan and purpose. This context gives meaning to all the events leading to the remarkable outpouring of praise and thanksgiving to God at Anne-Marie's funeral, while also sharpening the author's focus and direction for her own life and facilitating a closer bonding of the family unit.

Anne-Marie was truly a special child who continues to bring blessing to her family, her relatives and friends across Europe and the wider community in North Belfast as well as many individuals worldwide. I feel sure this book will help to spread this blessing which transcends traditional religious divides.

I feel honoured to have known Anne-Marie.

Brian C Craig
August 2005

Acknowledgements

My most grateful thanks go to my friends Majella and Kevin for their invaluable encouragement to write this book when it seemed a daunting project.

I am indebted to Suzanne for her perceptive and sensitive help with editing, to Therese and Colm for their untiring proofreading and to all my family members for giving me the time and space this project required.

Many thanks to you all!!

Johanna

Dedication

*I would like to dedicate this book
to the eternal love of God,
and to all those through whom I experience it most...*

*...my parents, my sister,
my Roland,*

*...my darling husband Pat,
our wonderful children
Martin Raphael, Pascal, Alma Lucy, John Patrick*

... Anne-Marie...

...and all my family in Christ.

*...and I would like to mention that
this book has been written to give Glory to God,
specifically in accordance with the following reading:*

Revelation 12, v. 11: "They overcame him...by the word of their testimony..."

Scripture is quoted with Isaiah 55 v. 11 in mind:

"...my word that goes out from my mouth: It will not return to me empty, but will accomplish what I desire and achieve the purpose for which I sent it."

Psalm 139 v. 16 *"All the days ordained for me were written in your book before one of them came to be."*

Preface

The story of Anne-Marie reaches into the realms of life before conception as well as life beyond death and includes the most wondrous circumstances surrounding her life on earth. My account of her life is accompanied by scripture quotations which are offered in an attitude of thanks and praise to God and in the hope of highlighting parallels to ancient spiritual truths.

Before Anne-Marie started to make herself known prior to her conception, telling me in a dream that she was our child, before any of the profoundly wonder-full things directly connected with her happened, in fact even before I was married or had any children at all, I once had an experience, which I want to include here for the sake of completeness, as I now think it was probably referring to Anne-Marie...

21 June 1990. It was my thirtieth birthday. Resting on my bed in the afternoon I drifted into dreamland for a while. Towards the end of my siesta I experienced a most unusual state of consciousness: I was not asleep, yet I was not fully awake. I was aware that I was lying there, my body strangely heavy.

With my eyes closed, I could plainly see light blue sky above me. A group of pigeons flew across the sky. As I watched, two pigeons separated themselves from the others. These two were flying, side by side, coming more into view above me. One of them changed in colour shape and size and became more and more brilliantly white, while at the same time filling out in size, nearly as if pregnant. It flew straight above me, by this time looking like a radiant heavenly being. From its centre - its chest, or its heart — rays of light streamed straight *into* my forehead. I was overwhelmed. My mouth had fallen open. I was left feeling both puzzled and blessed.

At that time I was engaged to be married, so I took the two pigeons to represent Pat and myself. I wondered if the ray of light was speaking of a child we might have at a later stage, who might be a blessing to me - and maybe also to others.

It was nearly six years later, with five and a half years of marriage and three children born to us in the meantime, that Anne-Marie made herself known (- again?) and prepared her way to joining our family in most unusual fashion...

Early Days

In the spring of 1996 I had a startling and powerful dream. In this dream a child of roughly three years of age repeatedly announced with total conviction: "I am your child". This child had certainly made up his or her mind that s/he wanted to come to us. Strangely, when I awoke I could not visualize the child anymore. All that was left with absolute clarity was the forcefully repeated proclamation: "I am your child."

This dream unsettled me. When I told Pat, my husband, about it, his reaction was: "One can dream many's a thing." Certainly my dream *alone* was not going to direct neither him nor me towards having another child. After all, we had three little ones already, two boys and a girl, and had decided that this was enough to be getting on with. Yet, the child's statement, put forward with such unshakable certainty, stayed in the forefront of my mind for quite a long time.

A few months later, one summer's day, I collected prints of a roll of film with snaps of our own children. Among our own photos I was greatly surprised to find two photographs - each in double edition - of a young baby whom I had never seen before. One of them showed the cheerfully smiling infant by itself in a baby's car seat, against a uniformly black background, while the other showed it together with a little boy with curly dark hair. Immediately the memory of the dream came flooding back, and I became inwardly stirred and excited.

Looking for a rational explanation, I wondered if Pat had gone to visit somebody, and photographed their baby. I looked through the negatives but found only those of our own children. I had to conclude that someone else's prints had been mixed up with our own. Certainly, that was what had happened, and yet the baby's photographs had appeared among ours for a *reason*. I am more and more convinced that *nothing* happens without reason.

The idea of adoption came to the fore but after some enquiries that avenue turned out to be a cul-de-sac. I was told we would not be accepted as adoptive parents as we had three children already and we were not unable to have another one ourselves. Yet the sense and awareness that there was a child trying to get through to us was more insistent now. In this situation even natural forms of birth control felt as though I was actively disallowing the life of this person, my child.

Matthew 18 v.5: "And whoever welcomes a little child like this in my name welcomes me."

On 14 December 1996 all three children were asleep early. The quiet evening was an unusual and welcome treat and I went to my John the Baptist icon to pray. Many years earlier my father had brought two identical sets of two posters advertising a Russian Orthodox icon exhibition back from Moscow. One was a print of an icon of Mary the Mother of Jesus and the other depicted St. John the Baptist[1]. My father had given one set to my sister and the other one to me.

I often prayed to Jesus Christ *through* St. John's icon, using it as a window to God and to focus my prayers. I had found that the position of his hands had signalled me to give things to him, to entrust him with all my concerns. Similarly, his eyes and the expression of his face conveyed what I felt were *his* views of my own position. I could have sensed a stern pulling-up, a reassuring warm welcome or a sorrowful acceptance of me, or sometimes his eyes were searching me for uprightness of heart, for honesty toward myself and God or for purity of intention.

That evening, something quite different happened. Instead of focusing on the image of St. John the Baptist, I gazed at the age-old cracked paint in the top right-hand corner of the icon and spotted the outline of a little child praying. Wearing a frilled hat and a layered dress, her hands held together in front of her face, she was positioned sideways, her face looking in the direction of St. John. The name 'Anne-Marie' was suddenly with me, and I wondered how best to spell it.

The image of this little girl stood out with such intensity and purpose that I went straight to Pat to ask him to look at it too. This was my first experience of this kind and I wanted verification. Pat wandered over to the icon. "Yes," he said, "I can see it too, and I've never seen it before."

Luke 1 v. 38: ""I am the Lord's servant," Mary answered, "May it be done to me as you have said.""

I felt strongly that it was the same child again praying to God to come to us, - the same child who had been in my dream and the same child who had brought herself back to mind through the photographs. Pat asked: "Do you really want to go through pregnancy and all that again?" I answered, "I don't want to stand in the way of God either." We sat down on the settee beneath the icon and talked and prayed about it. We came to the conclusion that we would give it just one chance - that night. If a child was to be conceived that night, it would confirm all the pointers; and if not, we would forget about all the occurrences.

The tangible blessing presence of God filled the house. Anne-Marie was conceived on 14 December 1996. Not a sound from any of the children. I had no doubt that night that I was pregnant.

Later that night we sat downstairs together and read the *Word of Life*[2]. The *Word of Life* for December 1996 had been the response of Mary the mother of Our Lord, to His annunciation by the Archangel Gabriel: *"let it be done onto me according to Thy word."* I felt perfectly in tune with the will of God.

Matthew 1v.25: "But he had no union with her until she gave birth..."

A great Peace, Joy and Love filled me that night. God was omnipresent, giving such lightness to my whole being that it seemed nothing less than natural for me to decide with joy and peace to keep this a "pure" pregnancy, a time of abstinence. Thankfully Pat was, even if a little hesitant at first, agreeable.

Psalm 139 v. 13 "For you created my inmost being; you knit me together in my mother's womb."

Remarkable things, which to my mind unmistakably point to Anne-Marie's great spiritual strength, happened during this pregnancy. For completeness sake I feel I must record some of them briefly...

Some people I was/we were in contact with during the pregnancy were touched in a powerful way by God, which left both me and them marvelling. It has to be noted that before

Anne-Marie had come to join us, this profound type of thing had not been happening among us.

An old school friend from Germany stayed with us over Christmas. Going through a difficult time after a break-up with her long-standing boyfriend she was feeling low. I tried to be with her in her pain, but came to realise that I was not able to give her any real hope outside my framework of reference: Christianity.

I remembered the Focolare[3]-style Christianity of communicating God through little acts of love, geared to what the other person can relate to (without mentioning the source - unless asked) as well as some Saint's advice: "Evangelise constantly, and if all else fails, also by using words," but even so, I did not really seem able to reach her until one day, when she wanted to know my alternative to despair.

After a *Lamb of God Community*[4] meeting Larry, the leader of the community, and I - and Anne-Marie - prayed with her. She experienced a great release of grace and of joy and gratitude to be granted this absolutely new beginning of faith.

That same winter, during Anne-Marie's earliest physical beginnings, Reyes our Spanish friend and godmother to our daughter Alma also came to stay with us. She, too, experienced a reverberating renewal of her faith, which continues bearing fruit now, over ten years later. Reyes was also deeply touched by the tangible unity in faith of the *Lamb of God Community;* by the sincerity with which members were sharing their struggles, insights, prophecies and experiences. She has since then worked for cross-denominational Christian unity in Spain not least by means of helping to shape some Christian radio programmes.

During Anne-Marie's life in utero, I was also involved for the first time in running an Alpha-*Course*[5] with *Shalom House*[6], and while I - and unborn Anne-Marie - were praying with one of the participants, this lady received her first vision, which contributed to her choosing to dedicate herself to Our Lord Jesus, and again, it was not a thing of fleeting nature. She is deeply involved to this day.

The *Lamb of God Community* is and has been a great treasure for me: my home. Located in North Belfast, a troubled area, it is...*a voice of one crying in the wilderness,...a light shining in the darkness,...*offering an oasis of praise of God, of silently waiting for Him, and of sharing and intercession. It is a unique set-up of ordinary Christian people from different denominational backgrounds.

As my pregnancy progressed, Anne-Marie often took an active part in the praise and worship. On occasions she was dancing for joy in utero during the singing. A number of people commented, how this pregnancy seemed to become me, and yes, instead of feeling tired and heavy and listless as with the previous three, I was flourishing, full of happiness and energy. This pregnancy was a source of great joy and strength to me.

But there were difficult times, too. In February 1997 I had a very bad flu. My entire body was aching; I had a high temperature and was coughing up green phlegm, day and night. I would have been given antibiotics if I had not been pregnant, but as it was, the doctor recommended lemon and honey. Many good people gave much good advice but the cough and flu stayed with me for weeks. I took some herbal cough mixture until I got frightened that it might damage the developing child, and maybe it did.

Wanting some reassurance that Anne-Marie was well in spite of the physical onslaught on me I tried to somehow get in contact with the child within. One day I received a faint "I'm fine" from her, which made me very happy, but it was an isolated occurrence.

Romans 8 v. 27: "...the Spirit intercedes for the saints in accordance with God's will."

One afternoon I was in bed with the flu and Pat was at home looking after the children. As everything was aching when I turned round in bed I made a few "ah" – "oh" – "ugh" sounds. Suddenly a powerful flow of words and sentences came out of my mouth. They were fully formed words and phrases or sentences of some language of which I had no knowledge. To me, it sounded a little like a mixture of an Indian language and Arabic. It took me by complete surprise and I was startled by the power and strength with which these words and sentences had flowed out of my mouth.

The doors of my room and those of the children's room were wide open, and although the children were making their own happy playing noises, I thought they might have heard me. So, in order not to worry them (i.e. "what on earth has gone wrong with mummy now?") I added a few funny noises at the end of these sentences, to make light of what had happened.

Immediately, I got my next surprise. One sentence passed through my head for a fraction of a second and, as I had not wilfully withheld my voice but had instead allowed the words to flow out of my mouth, to my utter bafflement I heard myself proclaim the following sentence: "Do not profane my prayers."

There was nothing left to say after this. It took me quite a while before I had recovered sufficiently to share this experience with anybody. I knew this was Jesus, telling me off for making funny noises after He had prayed His prayer of tongues through me.

Isaiah 49 v. 1: "Before I was born the Lord called me; ..."
Psalm 139 v.14: "...My frame was not hidden from you when I was made in the secret place..."

In retrospect, I now believe that Our Lord was praying for Anne-Marie. I have heard that it is around the eighth week of pregnancy that the intricacies of the heart are formed, and it would have been around that time that these things happened. I was filled with awe and reverence, and with a sense that the things which were happening with me and around me were far beyond my understanding.

The cry of Our Lord Jesus Himself, speaking in tongues on the cross, albeit interpreted, turned into an extraordinary experience during the springtime of 1997. Again, Anne-Marie was there, in utero.

I had not had it in mind to take a trip to Germany but as a friend needed a second adult to travel with her to qualify for special offer tickets, Pat volunteered to look after our three children to let me visit friends and relations in Germany before the arrival of our next baby. I had mapped out a busy schedule travelling up and down the country but felt that the most important stop would be with my cousin Roland and his family in Ludwigsburg.

My cousin Roland and I are like brother and sister. He awaited me on the platform while I stood behind the doors of the train, as it was rolling into the station. The train stopped, the doors opened, and there directly before me without needing to take a step to the right or the left stood Roland. The fine-tuning touch of our loving Lord was immediately tangible to both of us.

Sabine, Roland's wife, told me that she had felt a strange flutter of excitement about my coming, nearly like butterflies. There was a great sense of expectation in the air, yet things rolled on in a quiet and unspectacular manner.

We spent some time talking with each other, there was a lovely visit to a church with little Richard, their second son, but before long the second and last evening had come and nearly gone. Roland had said good-night and I was sitting up with Sabine when I thought of asking her if she would like to join with me in Pat's and my daily evening readings.

For some months Pat and I had taken some time every evening, to read chronologically a bit of the Gospel and a Psalm together. We continued with our readings while I was in Germany, for our nourishment and in order to remain in unity with each other. I had also asked Pat for his prayers especially for this stop.

Sabine was happy to join us in the readings. The Gospel reading told the story of Jesus on the cross crying out *"Eli Eli lama sabachtami"* (*"My God My God why have you forsaken me"*). This reading reminded me of how I had gained a better understanding of the meaning of 'Jesus forsaken' for my own life through the Focolare Movement, when I came to understand that Jesus did not only have first hand experience of the depths of desolation himself, feeling cut off both from God and from man, but that through this, I and all of us are now no longer alone in *our* cry of desperation, *"My God My God why have you forsaken me,"*

What I had *not* known was, that lying in her bed one night, quite to her own thorough unsettlement Sabine had let out a cry, *"My God My God why have you forsaken me,"* and that she had felt very guilty ever since, feeling both unworthy of uttering it and condemned for being blasphemous. The words of the Gospel reading, followed by the words I had added, had unlocked this experience, and allowed Jesus into her area of pain to administer healing. This, in turn, brought forth gushes of tears of overwhelming relief and joy.

Her longed-for first conscious meeting with her friend and Saviour, Jesus, was happening. She had awaited this moment from the time of her confirmation when their minister had told them about this moment coming at some stage in their lives.

Through the Spirit of God - the 'Giver of Life - who had made that reading the one for that day, and who had prompted me (us) to fly over, her outlook had changed. For long enough she had not had the strength to welcome the morning of a new day but the following morning for what seemed to her to be the first time ever, she was able to greet it with a decisive and sustained *__Yes!!!__*.

From Ludwigsburg I/we went on to Munich to visit two old school friends, never knowing that before too long we would see them all again under not quite the same circumstances. It was good to have made the effort to go down, even for reasons I was completely unaware of.

My first two National Health births had had their troubles and mishaps, so I went private for Alma's birth. This turned out to have been the right decision. Mr. White, our consultant, opted for bringing the section forward by a few days upon listening to my concerns, rather than relying solely on scans. And even though there were complications, and Alma had to go into neonatal intensive care for a little while, his decision had prevented further problems from arising. I was in no doubt under whose care my present pregnancy and birth of Anne-Marie should be.

At my first appointment Anne-Marie's entire pre-conception story just bubbled out of me with such joy and excitement that I did not immediately notice how Mr White had been listening with wide-eyed amazement and a half-opened mouth. He went on to do a scan and confirmed what I had described. "The icon was right," he said. Later, I brought the icon in for him to see and photocopied the top right hand corner with the child in it for him to keep. Reportedly he hung it up by his computer at home and his wife and family were equally interested and intrigued.

Anne-Marie's remarkable pre-conception story – especially the Russian Orthodox icon of John the Baptist as well as an unexpectedly renewed contact with an elderly Russian Orthodox lady, the late Tamara Korkashvili (a colleague of my father in days gone by), gave me the idea that Anne-Marie may be Russian Orthodox rather than Protestant or Roman Catholic. Wanting to facilitate this extraordinary child, I felt the need to explore the possibilities and implications of this thought.

I wrote to the Orthodox layman Mr. Adrian Crosby, who had built the only Russian Orthodox Church in Ireland (at that time) on his own grounds in the countryside in county Laois and told him of Anne-Marie's story. We arranged for me to visit Stradbally, near Portlaois, for Saturday evening Vespers and for Sunday Liturgy (28/29 June 1997) and to meet with Fr. Peter Baulk, a priest who came over once a month from England. I must have been quite a sight being not overly tall, heavily pregnant, and limping along with the help of a stick.

Fr. Peter pointed out some differences between Orthodox and other Christian practices and concluded that the decision whether the baby to be born was to be allowed to receive Orthodox baptism lay with his Bishop. He thought that in view of neither father nor mother being Orthodox, there might be some difficulties in assuring an Orthodox upbringing. Therefore his Bishop might be reluctant to agree to Orthodox baptism, even though there were remarkable and unusual circumstances which would seem to favour it. We stayed in contact by letters. No final decision was reached until after Anne-Marie was born.

After some persuasion a different Orthodox Priest, based in Dublin, eventually agreed to hold regular individual introductory teaching sessions about Orthodoxy for me once Anne-Marie would be born. Certainly Dublin was easier to reach than Stradbally, but due to Anne-Marie's poor health these meetings never came to pass.

Psalm 139 v. 16: "All the days ordained for me were written in your book before one of them came to be."

Eventually a date for Anne-Marie's caesarean section had to be set. The end of August was a likely time. In my family the 28th had been a date for dying and I hoped this date could be avoided. Mr. White immediately agreed to settle for a different date.

1 Corinthians 13 v.12: "Now I know in part; then I shall know fully, even as I am fully known."

Just allow me to say that I don't think of myself as a superstitious person. I know the love of God to be stronger than any other power in heaven or on earth. Yet I find there are a host of things that happen within the love of God which are beyond my understanding and ignoring these makes them no less real. Instead, it would remove me from the position of awe about the great mystery of God to one of reliance on my own knowledge and understanding, which, even if it were extraordinary would be limited by my being human and therefore remain necessarily incomplete.

Prior to the birth, I stayed overnight in hospital. All the usual tests were carried out and the midwives were particularly happy with the easy-to-find heartbeat, which they described as "loud and clear." Looking through some magazines to pass the time, I saw an article about a little boy who had heart problems. I felt sorry for him and for his family but did not really want to get too touched by it all. I turned over to the next page without reading the whole article…never knowing that before too long I would meet both him and his mother.

When the time finally came - and the injection of anaesthetic for my back was prepared - I had a compelling sense that this was all far too early. There should not have been any rush in getting this child born! My pains had eased during the course of the last week, and there was now no real reason to proceed with removing this little baby from its snug and safe hiding place so soon. I felt all this very strongly but the anaesthetic was ready. I had to go with it. I took Pat's hand and we started to pray the 'Our Father' together, putting all in God's hands.

Extraordinarily, the *Word of Life* for the month of August 1997 was nearly an immediate follow-up to the passage from December 1996. It was again from the first chapter of St. Luke's Gospel. Mary's words were on this occasion uttered in response to the words of her relation Elisabeth, the mother of St. John the Baptist, who had said of her (Luke 1, v.45): *"Blessed is she who has believed that what the Lord has said to her will be accomplished!"* Mary had responded with the Magnificat: *"…for he has been mindful of the humble state of his servant. From now on all generations will call me blessed…"* (Luke 1,v.48).

Exodus 34 v. 29: "…he was not aware, that his face was radiant…"

The anaesthetic was given and the doctors were working at the section behind a screen. Anne-Marie began to cry as soon as only her head was lifted out. When she was fully born I saw a sheen of joy all over Pat's face. There was a radiance. When it was

announced that a little girl had been born, he said to me: "You were right all along."

Anne-Marie was grunting with each breath and breathing quite fast. She was taken from my side for this reason. Thankfully Pat was there, to go with her, so I did not fret and worry too much, but unlike after my previous two sections I did not allow myself to drift off to sleep properly. I had to be kept near the operating theatre for a certain length of time for observation. When I was allowed up to the ward where Pat and Anne-Marie were, Pat still had a radiance on his face. He told me that they had not weighed her until after she had relieved herself, but even at that, she weighed 3360g or 7.6 lb. He told me they were keeping her in the nursery to keep an eye on her breathing. We agreed he should go to ring people.

Matthew 28 v.19: "...go and make disciples of all nations baptising them in the name of the Father and of the Son and of the Holy Spirit.."

When he came back after that, the sheen on his face had disappeared. He was looking concerned. Apparently the oxygen saturations had dropped and Anne-Marie was receiving oxygen in an incubator. Transfer plans were made for her to go to the Neonatal Intensive Care Unit (NICU) of the Royal Victoria Hospital. As soon as I heard of transfer plans I requested to be transferred to the "Royal" as well.

We were waiting for the ambulance for Anne-Marie when I asked the midwife/nurse who was attending us if she would baptize Anne-Marie. She was delighted to do me this favour although she said that there would probably be enough time to get the hospital chaplain. The knowledge that emergency baptisms by lay-Christians are acceptable to the Churches and my sense of urgency, as well as the delight on the midwife's face about my request, made me decide in favour of the nurse going ahead.

Luke 2 v.21: "...he was named Jesus, the name the angel had given him before he had been conceived."

I was put into a wheelchair with drip attachment and the little "ceremony" took place in the nursery. The nurse had a small amount of water in a little aluminium foil dish, and after enquiring about the baby's full name, she poured a little drop of the water over Anne-Marie's head saying "I baptize you in the name of Anne-Marie Angela." - I said nothing, as the nurse was so happy although I would have been happier if she had said "I baptize you in the name of the Father, the Son and the Holy Spirit, and give you the name of Anne-Marie Angela."

Not long after that Anne-Marie was whisked away, and I spent what seemed an eternity waiting for my transfer ambulance to the Royal Maternity Hospital, where I was admitted to the postnatal ward nearest the Neonatal Intensive Care Unit (NICU).

Four hours passed before I saw Anne-Marie again. Somebody wheeled me over to see her in the NICU. She was put into my arm properly for the first time and a nurse took a Polaroid photograph of us. There is something so lovely about holding your new baby. A wave of love came over me.

Apparently she had got over her worst time so far, when the oxygen saturations of her blood had dropped dangerously low and she had turned blue. Thankfully, by the time she had arrived in the NICU her saturations were back within a normal range. The nurses were keeping a very close eye on her and she was attached to a monitor which displayed her heart rate and oxygen saturation and other details which I couldn't take in on the first day even though our nurse explained everything very patiently and caringly.

Pat found us there, after arranging for someone to baby-sit at home, and it was good for us three to be together again. I did not like to leave Anne-Marie to go to my own ward, but there was nothing more that could be done to bring us closer together and I was thankful I had got a ward immediately below the intensive care unit. I told the staff that I should like to try to feed Anne-Marie myself. That night a nurse from the ICU came looking for a drop of milk from me. I was glad I had brought a hand-pump with me but the results were anything but spectacular: just a few drops, half of them getting wasted during the transfer into a drinking bottle.

From the next morning onwards I made my way up to the ICU to breastfeed and after a day or two it started to go very well. In accordance with my request, I was called up by the nurses whenever Anne-Marie wakened, day or night. I would hasten up, sometimes walking more and sometimes less upright, delighted none the less to be able to be with her and to try to feed her. Once or twice I woke up immediately prior to the phone call coming down to my ward, which was very reassuring for me. It showed me that we had a good mother-baby connection with each other even in spite of our physical distance.

Even though Alma had paved the way for getting to know the neonatal intensive care unit it was quite a place. Incubators and monitors; *bleep bleep bleep bleeps* of various pitches coming from all over the room, bright lights, and somewhere in the middle of it all, little tiny human beings at various stages of fighting for their lives.

All members of staff were very special caring people. Parents were allowed to visit anytime and they also allowed Anne-Marie's brothers and sister in. When visiting, the three of them were sitting on high stools along one side of the incubator, gazing in amazement and with

great interest at their new baby sister. The little ditty in answer to any questions about their ages went: "They are six, four, two and new."

Mr. White phoned the Unit from his holiday resort to enquire about how things were going. One day he even surprised us by appearing in person, even though we were now under the care of the Royal Victoria Hospital, and just as he was speaking to us Anne-Marie gave a little smile. I was very surprised about this, at such a tender age. Mr. White suggested she may have recognised his voice. I kept looking for another little smile, but it had been a one-off.

He said, a little probingly, that this place (meaning the NICU) was probably one of the last places I would have expected to find myself in. This reminded me of the curious fact that during this pregnancy, whenever anybody asked: "Well, what would you rather have this time, a wee boy or a wee girl?" I had answered, as usual, that I did not really mind. But when they in turn completed my answer by saying "That's right, so long as it's healthy", contrary to my habitual agreement to this during previous pregnancies, I had usually continued on saying: "Even if it's not healthy I'll still have to love it."

When, prior to her birth, I had recounted Anne-Marie's pre-conception story to the Lamb of God Community, Kevin Gault had had a premonition about there being a health problem with Anne-Marie. Understandably, he had not wanted to say anything about it at that stage. Now, while we were in hospital, he and Susan, also a community member and neighbour, came to our house and prayed with and for Pat and the older children as well as for Anne-Marie and me. The Lamb of God Community has been a tower of strength, a source of unceasing prayer for Anne-Marie and me throughout all our difficult times, and we were noticeably carried by the Presence, Grace and Mercy of God. I could not dare to imagine how different everything would have been without this.

One day Anne-Marie was deemed well enough to have her first bath in the NICU. Someone brought a stand and a baby bath filled with lovely warm water and said I could bath her today.

Still having a slight niggle in my mind about the somewhat incomplete baptism of the first day, I immediately thought I should seize this opportunity to put my mind at ease. I decided to conduct a very simple little 3x immersion ceremony, in accordance with my understanding of Orthodox baptisms except for not risking a total immersion under the circumstances. I did this quietly, not speaking audibly but speaking in my spirit: *"I baptize you in the name of the Father"* – while very gently lowering her into the bath until the water level reached up to her neck and out again, *"and of the Son"*, in and out in the same fashion, *"and of the Holy Spirit"*- in and out. *"Amen."* Followed by a gentle, careful rub-a-dub-dub in the ready-and-waiting towel on my lap.

It was lovely and prayerful and indeed happy, too. I was delighted that this opportunity had arisen, and that I had taken it.

It had been one of those occasions on which the Love, Joy and Peace of God had become one single tangible entity. Nobody around us was any the wiser, as it had been a silent ceremony, but I think we both, or should we say all three of us, not forgetting God, enjoyed it.

During one of Anne-Marie's very early morning feeds in the NICU, we first heard the news of Princess Diana's accident, and then of her death over the radio, which was playing in the background. It seems an odd coincidence that Diana died soon after Anne-Marie's birth, while Anne-Marie later died in Princess Diana's Children's Hospital in Birmingham, and was subsequently laid to rest in a cemetery situated along *Prince Charles Way*...

An appointment with Clark Clinic, the pediatric cardiology ward (children's heart ward) over in the Royal Belfast Hospital for Sick Children had been made. Pat and I accompanied the porter who came to take Anne-Marie in her incubator over to be seen by her paediatric consultant cardiologist, Dr Brian Craig. Her echo-scan showed up substantial congenital (born-with) heart problems. Lots of medical terminology came our way.

At this first encounter with Dr. Craig I was deeply touched by his considerate manner. He painstakingly ensured that we knew everything we might want to know. He was there for us, explaining things twice over voluntarily; at one stage even crouching on the floor while explaining things, so that I could see him while I was breastfeeding in a low chair.

He spoke of Anne-Marie having the potential to have a fairly normal life with the condition called Anatomically Corrected Transposition of the Great Arteries. It has to be said though, that on the first day not all the diagnostic findings, especially the valve-problems, had been available to him.

He spoke of a medium size hole and said that one can sometimes find that these grow over by themselves. It was mainly a matter of "wait and see and keep an eye on her" at this stage. He also said he would admit Anne-Marie to Clark Clinic for further cardiac observation. However, as Anne-Marie had not shown any signs of irregular heartbeat up in the NICU and as her oxygen saturations were fine he kindly decided to delay admission until I had been discharged myself from the postnatal ward so that I could continue to breastfeed her directly without having to use the pump, and without having to freeze and defrost and transport the milk across from one part of the hospital to another.

After this, our first contact with Clark Clinic, Anne-Marie and I both returned to our previous wards for another few days. Strangely, I was not too upset by everything that had happened. It all happened at such breathtaking speed that it seemed to take all my energy to keep up mentally with understanding what was happening. In those very early days I saw the whole situation as a gift through which to grow.

I was reminded of the Focolare Movement's teaching of living the present moment, and remember remarking to a friend on the phone how I could not imagine a better teacher of living the present moment, than a child whose next moment one cannot predict.

Anne-Marie's "Anatomically Corrected Transposition of the Great Arteries" meant that there was some "back-to front plumbing." The smaller pumping heart chamber, which in the normal person pumps used (blue) blood to and through the lungs for absorbing oxygen, had to supply the much larger systemic circulation. That is, it had to pump red, oxygenated blood around the body. Conversely, the chamber which structurally speaking should have done this more demanding work was "plumbed" to supply the smaller pulmonary (lung) circulation.

In addition to these findings a second echo-study revealed that Anne-Marie also had

- a hole between her upper heart chambers (these are the chambers which receive an inflow of blood; one side receiving used blood from around the body, and the other side receiving oxygenated blood from the lungs). It meant that there was a danger of "fresh" and "used" blood getting mingled.
- a hole between the lower (pumping) heart chambers also representing a danger of mingling used and fresh blood.
- a narrowing of the artery to her lungs (pulmonary artery).
- a regurgitating heart valve (leaking blood back into the lungs at every beat). This turned out to be the biggest problem.

-   an enlarged heart. In order to cope with the extra demands made on Anne-Marie's heart it had increased its muscle-bulk, which in the case of the heart is not desirable as it can lead to further problems.

A young doctor in the NICU thought it was quite amazing to think that even with all the different plumbing defects, holes, narrowing of the pulmonary artery and regurgitation at the valve, the pressure in her heart was balanced out so perfectly - apart from the first few hours after her birth - that Anne-Marie was able to maintain normal oxygen saturations (in the upper 90s). There was no blue colouring to be seen anywhere: pink nail beds, pink lips and tongue; in fact she looked perfectly healthy, chubby and contented. Thinking back to that time now I think in my own mind that it is truly something to marvel and wonder about. Should she 'by rights' not have died on the first day?

John 16 v.33: "In this world you will have trouble. But take heart! I have overcome the world."

Clark Clinic

After my discharge from the maternity ward Anne-Marie and I came to Clark Clinic where we were given a little side ward to afford us some privacy for breast feeding. Anne-Marie was on a monitor, which meant that I had to be mindful of her attachments when lifting or cuddling her. I was tired from the section, from the breast-feeding-nights and from trying to adjust to - and make sense of - the new situation. Our side ward was small and impossible to air properly, but I felt just as though we had been given a piece of the Garden of Eden: for the first time Anne-Marie and I were allowed to be together continually. I was delighted.

This experience of bliss lasted only for a short time. All too soon Dr. Craig came and explained that because of a leaking valve they had discovered in a recent echo-scan they now wanted to start Anne-Marie on Digoxin, a heart medicine designed "to help her heart squeeze better" and on Spironolactone and Frusemide (diuretics) to prevent her lungs from retaining fluid. Although he was no less friendly than before it was clear from his tone of voice that this was a final decision and that there could be no discussion about it.

It was as if a bombshell had hit me. I was in turmoil.

Modern medicine and faith had not met within me on this scale before, and were at complete loggerheads with each other, throwing me into confusion and helplessness.

Was my Lord, who had made Anne-Marie and who had balanced out the pressures in her heart against all the odds going to need help in his job, from Frusemide and Spironolactone? I just could not believe that He did. The idea of giving the medicines to our special little Anne-Marie, with whom the Hand of the Lord had been from *before* her physical beginning, seemed to me to be like making a statement of distrust to my Lord. Had He not done everything so perfectly up to now, keeping her well, when by rights she should have died? ... Keeping her pink, feeding well, looking healthy?

Quite apart from that, although it has to be said that this was not the main hurdle, I had never liked modern chemical medicines. I preferred alternatives which are closer to nature and milder, such as homeopathic medicines.

Isaiah 38 v.17: "Surely it was for my benefit that I suffered such anguish"

Up to this point, I had not had real difficulties with the whole situation. Visitors to the maternity ward had often remarked how difficult it must be without Anne-Marie, among all the other mums with their babies beside them. Yet I had always been able to reassure them that I was fine and that all things happened for a reason.

But now things were very different. Nobody seemed to sense or to understand the turmoil I was in. I do not remember if I actually cried before this point, but I do remember not being able to stop my tears when the nurse came into our side ward to show me how to administer the medicines. I tried to apologise, saying that it was quite something to have to get used to - this idea of giving medicines.

The nurse comforted me, saying that because they give medicines to nearly all their patients it had become so commonplace to them that they were not always aware of the impact this turn of events had on a parent. She was allowing my tears. I could not talk to her about my inner turmoil, but she was soothing to be with. However, it nearly broke my heart to watch how my lovely defenceless little baby was fed these disgusting tasting chemicals by syringe (of course without a needle) into her unsuspecting little mouth. I spent all my coins at the phone box in the corridor at the end of Clark Clinic. That phone has heard so many parents cry ...

Isaiah 32 v.2: "...man will be like a shelter from the wind and a refuge from the storm, like streams of water in the desert and the shadow of a rock in a thirsty land."

I was on the phone to Pat to tell him the news about the medication and to pour out my heart. As always, he was there to listen, to support, to love, ready to receive the jumbled thoughts of my raw heart, to allow them and then, where possible, to gently map out the way forward. Although it was not welcome news for him either and he did not take it lightly, he suggested that "'they' must know *something* of what they are doing" and carefully advised to go along with the medication even if *I* was not convinced about it. He said "let it be on *my* head" meaning, that if there was any guilt of lack of faith to be attached to this decision, this guilt should fall on him rather than on me. Without this selfless act of substitution I may very well not have been able to go ahead.

My sister also said something that made me more able to tolerate the idea of the medicines. She said that Anne-Marie may have chosen this particular time to come to us with her physical problems, especially *because* she was aware that modern medical treatments would be available.

The day Anne-Marie got her first dose of the medicines was followed by the first night that I could not get her settled. Again and again she was drawing up her little legs as if she had a sore tummy. She was restless and agitated and just could not relax. Perhaps she was also aware of my inner tension although I tried to be calm and reassuring for her. As I could not get her settled in the sideward, I turned into a night-wanderer having disconnected her from her monitor, walking up and down the length of the ward holding her close to me, but she would not settle.

I explained to the nurses that Anne-Marie had never been like this before, and that I thought it was due to the medications. But rather than conceding that the medications could be reviewed or changed or withdrawn, which of course was what I had really wanted to hear, they tried to reassure me, explaining that it could take a couple of days before she would get used to them. As a last resort, they offered to have her written up for Paracetamol or some other medication above and beyond what she had been given already "to settle her down for the night." Of course, they were being helpful, and in fairness could not have said anything else, but I just could not help thinking and feeling that this was all wrong. I felt alone in an alien world which operated according to a different agenda from mine.

Hebrews 11 v. 13: "And they admitted that they were aliens and strangers on earth."

I was like a recluse in my side ward, thankful for the privacy it afforded and happy to have little or no contact with the outside world. I did not see eye to eye with it and did not want to bridge the gap. It felt like a hostile world out there which had no room for the likes of Anne-Marie and me the way we were. The outer world at large, as experienced through the junk mail Pat brought in for me among personal letters, sickened me to a hitherto unknown degree.

Matthew 6v.24: "You cannot serve both God and Money."

Fashions, beauty products, fast cars, settees... advertised appealing to the ultimate worldly virtue of apparently saving money while in the process of spending it. With new clarity I could see the desperate emptiness of this money-god, which so easily holds us in its spell. How is it that the implied promise of happiness through perpetually acquiring new things so easily lures us into denial and rejection of our true nature as creatures made in the image and likeness of God? ...As such creatures surely we have no need for proving ourselves by the clothes we wear, by the hairstyle we have, or by the car or the settee we use. Instead, are we not just here for the benefit of others and for the Glory of God?

All these age-old realizations hit me with resounding new vigor and transparency. Anne-Marie's very being effortlessly polarized the two worlds for me and completely stripped all credibility from material striving. I was grateful to be allowed to withdraw from our usual western world for a while.

Bit by bit I got used to the concept of the medicines and was able to administer them myself. I found it helpful to say a prayer while giving them, asking Our Lord to bless them, to bless Anne-Marie, and to allow the medicines to help her towards health.

We were discharged on Friday 5 September 97. It was good to get home. Being back was quite an experience: I was a wanted woman! Three young children and one special little baby wanted me. Visitors wanted me, the health visitors and midwives came, also wanting my time; there were dinners to be made, homework to be supervised, quarrels to be sorted out, children to get fed, washed, dressed and changed, Anne-Marie to be attended to. I was tired from the caesarean birth, the wound of which had got infected by this stage, and from the 24 hour shifts. Some things like tidying up and cleaning simply did not get done.

Luke 10 v.41, 42: ""Martha, Martha," the Lord answered, "you are worried and upset about many things, but only one thing is needed." "

I coped by dealing with priorities only and did not allow the rest to irritate me too much. When we went back to hospital for Anne-Marie's weight check, I even got some praise from one of the ward-sisters because Anne-Marie had put on a little weight. We were allowed to go home again. It was encouraging. I was hopeful that things would go well from here. I had no idea of what lay ahead.

Psalm 34 v.5: "Those, who look to him are radiant"

When Anne-Marie was about two and a half weeks old I was sitting on the settee under the same icon of St. John the Baptist, through which she had been announced. I was in the middle of feeding her when to my absolute amazement she turned her head towards the icon, looked at it, and gave it the loveliest, biggest, long-lasting radiant smile! At that age! I am told babies usually do not smile until they are about eight weeks old.

What was I to make of this extraordinary event? There was obviously a connection between Anne-Marie and the icon which had caused her to transcend the usual pattern of things, and caused her to give this beautiful smile. It felt to me, as though it was a smile of joyful recognition and remembrance of the icon, through which she had entered into our lives. It seemed to say, "Yes, look, and I'm here now!" I was astounded and elated. This special child continued to be special even *after* she was born.

Mathew 6 v.22 "The eye is the lamp of the body. If your eyes are good, your whole body will be full of light."

Anne-Marie always had very knowing eyes. A friend of ours who had once come to visit, on seeing Anne-Marie took a step backwards and exclaimed in honest surprise "She looks wise!"

My cousin Roland, himself a doctor, put it this way: "She appears to have brought with her a fully developed conscience", and he was able to say this from viewing photographs I had sent him.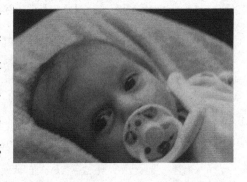

A swift reminder of how delicately balanced Anne-Marie's heart was came one Saturday. I had fed her and tried to bring up her wind for a while. There had been a little vomit - nothing too much out of the ordinary. I was giving her a complete change as her clothes had got a little soiled. She was lying on her back when I noticed her little fingers and toes going blue.

I looked at this in disbelief rather than alarm. I wanted to rub my eyes and look again. As I was dialing 999 for an emergency ambulance to the hospital, there was a sense of rising panic. I tried to stay cool. Pat was away in the country with the car as he usually is on a Saturday. He had taken Raphael with him and had left Pascal and Alma with me. I urged them to get their coats and shoes on while getting Anne-Marie into her clothes.

I thought Anne-Marie had colder hands and feet than usual. I thought maybe she just went blue because I had taken her clothes off, and she had got cold. Yet, our house was very warm and it had never happened before. Maybe, I thought, a little of her vomit might have been breathed in, and interfered with the absorption of oxygen. Somehow I blocked out the possibility that it could be due to her heart problems. Had they not said at the hospital that if things were to get worse it would be a gradual process, probably taking a couple of days?

The ambulance arrived and at the same time Anne-Marie regained her normal colour. Alma and Pascal were frightened by the strange happenings and did not want to go into the ambulance, but did not want to let go of me either. The crew urged us to hurry. Miriam, our next-door neighbour, appeared and thank God quickly assessed the situation correctly. She coaxed Alma and Pascal into staying with her, promising them a children's video. On the way to the hospital Anne-Marie was given oxygen and when we arrived at the Children's Hospital Anne-Marie was perfectly pink. We were allowed home after a doctor had seen us.

I got in contact with priests and ministers of different churches for the purpose of arranging a suitable ceremony for "churching" a child who had been "sort-of" baptised twice over. My first choice had been the Orthodox Church but eventually we were informed that the Archbishop would not allow it, if Anne-Marie was going to be brought up outside the context of having at least one Orthodox parent and one Orthodox godparent. He apparently also thought that there would be too much confusion if there were Catholic, Protestant and Orthodox Christians all in one family. I could understand his concern, although I also thought that it would offer an opportunity of unity across the Christian divides. I felt that if it were possible to allow Christians of the different traditions to flourish through the love of God within our family setting, then it should also be possible worldwide. *"May they all be one"* (John 17).

Mark 10 v. 14: "He said to them, "Let the little children come to me, and do not hinder them, for the kingdom of God belongs to such as these...." "

In retrospect I still feel that Anne-Marie would have been helped on her short journey through life on earth if she had been able to partake in the Eucharist – a Sacrament which only in the Orthodox Church is available to baptized children and babies.

The next weighing session at the hospital showed Anne-Marie to be underweight. I was feeling guilty, that maybe I had not taken enough time and care over feeding Anne-Marie, but ward sister Alison Kearney reassured me saying, "most babies, in fact nearly all babies, … yes, I would go as far as to say *all* babies with congenital heart disease have to have a calorie supplement at some stage or other." The reason for this is that their defective hearts use up a lot of extra energy above and beyond that of a healthy heart. In addition most heart-children also take less milk than normal as they have less appetite and less sucking power.

A dietician gave us the calorie-wonder-powder, Duocal, which had to be mixed with Anne-Marie's milk. This sounded quite straightforward, but in actual fact more than doubled the feeding time. Since the powder could not be added when breastfeeding, "feeding" would mean pumping off milk, then adding the powder, and then bottle feeding it. That meant spending half an hour pumping off and half an hour feeding, followed by cleaning and sterilizing for pump and bottles. Feeding time was every three hours, which meant that *more than one* out of three hours was filled up with it.

I was always hoping that there would be no squeamish or embarrassed visitors arriving as pumping time came round, for whose sake Anne-Marie might have needed to wait just that little bit longer for her meal…. Anne-Marie of course would always have welcomed this. She was in no particular rush to get fed. In fact, Anne-Marie would have been very happy if it had been possible to live here on earth without ever having to eat at all. She fed more or less willingly at that stage, whenever she was offered it, but never cried for food. I could not rely on her to indicate the arrival of feeding-time in the same way as I had done with my other three children. I had to be wholly responsible for keeping up the prescribed routine, living at all times with one eye on the clock, even at night time when I had to set and re-set the alarm.

Tiredness had become a way of life for us. Once or twice I woke up about two hours after one of the night-feed alarms had gone off, lying down with my feet on the floor and the blankets pulled back. I had fallen back to sleep in the process of getting up. Even using a number of alarm clocks did not always do the trick. Pat was attending to Raphael, Pascal and Alma during the nights (toilet runs, coughs, bad dreams or other little disturbances) and I was looking after Anne-Marie every few hours. I used to go up the stairs with my eyes closed during the day, just in order to give them that little extra rest they were craving.

I remember one day a friend was visiting. I had just finished pumping off milk for Anne-Marie and gave Pat some detailed instructions as to what to do with it - which bottle to take out of the sterilizer, which cap to use, etc.- and concluded my instructions by saying "and then put it in the bin" (!) (…meaning in the fridge).

My friend knew from first hand experience how tiredness could jumble up one's thinking. Her own daughter, whom she had also been breast feeding as long as possible, is disabled, and especially in the earlier days required plenty of hospital trips. It was on one of those hospital trips, during the final check if all necessary items were on board the car before setting off, that her overtired husband asked if she had remembered to take her breasts with her. We were laughing till the tears came to our eyes.

Anne-Marie's feeding regime also meant that I had to forego or cut short my Wednesday evenings at the Lamb of God Community, although these meetings were essential for my own well being. But thankfully, when I heard about Vassula Ryden[7] coming to the Waterfront Hall here in Belfast, I managed to attend some of it with Anne-Marie. It was the first time I encountered this Greek Orthodox lady prophet, ablaze with the Spirit. During the rushed individual prayer time after the main address, both the Russian Orthodox priest who accompanied her on her journeys and Vassula herself prayed over me rather than Anne-Marie, but by now I am convinced that their prayers helped both of us.

Through time Anne-Marie became a very poor feeder, eventually taking only small amounts and at frequent intervals. As with her first medicines, I could not help being suspicious about the effect of Duocal on her appetite. I had also found that if I succeeded in giving her more than just the usual *one* ounce per feed, she would be prone to vomiting, which I thought was best avoided.

Even without having any scales at home I knew that things were not looking good. I feared that Anne-Marie would need to be admitted after the next weighing. Everything inside me was rebelling. I felt like a bucking horse, refusing to go the inevitable way and wanting to jump and gallop in the opposite direction. I felt like picking up my Anne-Marie and running away with her, far, far away from all hospitals. I felt like taking the next aeroplane to Germany with her, anything, anything but to have to be admitted.

Anne-Marie was about seven weeks old, when she was admitted with "failure to thrive". Her weight had fallen hopelessly outside all normal weight-chart percentiles. She weighed more or less her birth weight now. In the olden days, before the age of echo-scans and high-tech equipment, I suppose she would have died of "consumption."

The love and compassion shown by Anne-Marie's consultant, Dr. Craig, immediately melted all my inner resistance. In his presence I freely acknowledged that Anne-Marie had to be admitted to hospital. He was so alive to the happenings of every moment. He shared the disappointment of Pat having nearly used up all his holidays. He seemed to enjoy observing Anne-Marie and commented upon the way in which she looked at her mummy. He welcomed Anne-Marie and entered into a relationship with her.

On one occasion when he came to our side ward, just as I was administering the medicines, he greeted Anne-Marie and talked to her, giving her his undivided attention as if speaking to a much older person: "Hello, Anne-Marie, are you taking your Digoxin?" He was showing such love and respect for her, even though she was "only" a tiny baby, that it became evermore easier for me to accept our situation. The way this man relates to all people around him, whether patients or parents, domestics, doctors or nurses is in itself a teaching, a meditation on humanity, on humility, on gentleness and on Christianity alive.

Sr. Alison Kearney was the other key person for us. What a wonderful angel we had been given in her! She understood where I was at and she knew without any explanations who I was. She knew that I felt responsible for Anne-Marie and she did not try to take over. She knew that I instinctively felt afraid of Anne-Marie being sucked into the hospital apparatus, afraid of her loosing her young identity, of her turning into a case-history handled by everyone rather than being my very special individual darling daughter, gift of God.

She understood that it was more important to me to be with Anne-Marie than to get a breakfast or a dinner. She knew I would appreciate getting what was left over from the ward dinners, and unobtrusively she made sure that untouched leftovers came my way. She knew that she had to be in a position of trust for us to work comfortably together for Anne-Marie's sake, and she was, like none other, able to establish this trust.

And there was a lot I had to learn from her. I had come thinking that I knew a thing or two about feeding babies, as this was my fourth one. However, in the light of Sr. Alison's experience I had to adjust my thinking very quickly. I might have known how to feed a hungry baby, but I certainly knew nothing about feeding babies with no appetite. Resistance to being fed was no longer to stop my feeding efforts and I learnt to resume the feeding immediately after a vomit. This required extra milk. Aptamil formula milk was introduced and breast milk phased out. Anne-Marie was also very windy and bringing up her wind was difficult. The whole picture certainly added up to one very hard to feed little girl, in need of professional help.

The x-ray showed congestion of the lungs and Anne-Marie was started on Captopril, which had to be gradually increased to the full dosage. It would widen the smaller blood vessels in the arms and legs, (dilate the peripheral blood vessels), and would thus relieve some of the burden off the heart. Hopefully this would bring back the appetite.

During this admission everything centred on whether Anne-Marie's milk intake would improve. Dr Craig went on his holidays, and so Dr Casey, another consultant, came to talk to me together with Sr. Alison. He told me that an operation would become inevitable if there was no improvement in Anne-Marie's feeding. He also explained that they would really prefer not to have to operate on one so young and small, as there would be a high risk attached to the operation.

John 16 v. 20: "...you will weep and mourn while the world rejoices. You will grieve, but your grief will turn to joy."

This was hard to take in. I remember distinctly that during this time I decided, that if ever I won a substantial amount of money, I would donate it to Clark Clinic for a parents' crying room, padded and lockable from inside.

Genesis 43 v.30: "Joseph hurried out and looked for a place to weep."

I felt the need to cry, not just to sit there with tears in my eyes, or tears rolling down my cheeks, I wanted to wail, to howl, to cry out with all my soul. I wanted to be able to throw myself on the floor and allow my body to be jerking to the sound of my anguish, flowing unchecked until it would subside, after hours.

I became acutely aware of the fact that Anne-Marie might only have been given to us for a short time. This had a number of consequences. For the first time ever I tried to properly learn the workings of an elaborate and excellent SLR camera, which we had been given seven years earlier as a wedding present. Photography became something of a passion. I was not going to be short of photographs of Anne-Marie, if that was all we might have left of her soon.

Also, there was no time to lose. The time to love her was *now*, because there might not be a later-on. Loving her and being there for her became a thing of even greater importance and urgency than ever before. I sang little 'Anne-Marie'-ditties to her, like: (To the tune *Oh Rosemary I love you*)

"Oh Anne-Marie, I love you,

I'm always thinking of you …"

(Repeat unceasingly)

I loved being with her day and night, begrudging the time a bath for me or a visit to the toilet would take. Anne-Marie's condition put all my other worries and concerns into perspective. They meant nothing: none of them were life threatening.

It also put me in touch with my understanding of death. It was clear to me, that God was intimately involved in every aspect of Anne-Marie's life. I did not fear death for her sake; I was certain that she would go straight back into the arms of God.

I felt I could accept it from His hand if He wanted her back. I was sure that if He wanted to take her back so soon, He had very good reasons, even if I was not going to be able to understand them just at this point. This gave me a peace which was frequently stronger than my anxieties.

Every now and then my brain seemed too small to cope with all the many thoughts it was trying to process. There were a lot of thoughts, feelings and worries, but there was nothing much one could *do*. Either she would start feeling better again or she would not.

Things looked bad enough for Sr. Alison to eventually come and have a chat with me about force-feeding Anne-Marie through a tube in her nose. She introduced the topic very sensitively, saying that she disliked this option as it was such an unnatural thing to do but also mentioned how she thought that it might offer Anne-Marie the chance to have a restful night; to sleep through the night, while getting fed effortlessly. She took me to see a number of other babies on the ward who had a tube fitted and seemed to be quite unperturbed by it. In the face of a high-risk operation it seemed a good option to me.

In retrospect I can only say that I am glad that I did not know what lay before us when I agreed to have Anne-Marie force-fed. We had decided to make it a slow continuous feed to avoid her vomiting up boluses, which could have been too voluminous for her, as vomiting with a tube in place is not always straightforward. Sr. Alison had been on day shift, so when the night shift took over, a nurse put a tube through Anne-Marie's nose into her stomach, and secured it onto her cheek with sticky plaster.

It wasn't so much Anne-Marie's cries of pain that got to me when the tube was inserted as the look of terror on her face. Her cries and the look in her eyes were those of a person being subjected to an unprovoked violation of their human dignity. She conveyed to me a sense of outrage, upset and disbelief that we had so totally misjudged her sensitivity and awareness of what was happening to her.

Had we really expected that she should be able to just let this be done and then go to sleep as if nothing had happened? She was thoroughly upset and could not be appeased. The only place where she would half-settle was on my arm. There was no restful sleep in sight, no getting used to it, no giving over.

Eventually, I put her in her buggy and wheeled it up and

down a foot or two, as this was the total distance allowed by the length of the feeding-tube. In this way she went up a bit and down a bit alongside my bed in the side ward most of the night. Restless and making grunting noises, Anne-Marie kept trying to wipe away the tube, while the relentless machine continually dribbled in the milk. The nurses were acting on instructions left and were not in a position to change arrangements.

Sometime in the middle of the night, the machine's milk container was empty and had to be replaced. The new container was put up and the mindless machine started up again. In the dim light of my side ward I spotted an air bubble which was slowly, slowly winding its way through the spiraling connecting tube up toward where it met Anne-Marie's nose. Anne-Marie had problems with her wind and I thought one should try not to aggravate them.

I drifted in and out of drowsy sleep trying to keep an eye on the painfully slow advance of the bubble. Eventually I asked a nurse if she would not mind letting the air out for us. She found the idea funny, saying that this was a very small amount of air in comparison to the amounts we swallow during normal feeding. Of course, she was right...

I was glad to see the morning come and with it Sr. Alison, the impersonation of hope, of innovative ideas and of sound advice. The exercise was proclaimed unsuccessful. It took *more than a day* after her naso-gastric tube had been removed for Anne-Marie to stop grunting.

Sr. Alison left no stone unturned in trying to get her to take more milk. She introduced different teats, different temperatures of milk, different compositions of milk and Duocal, and most importantly she also applied her great experience when *positioning* Anne-Marie during feeding. She used her fingers to gently push in Anne-Marie's wee cheeks so that there would be the chance of a better suck while ever so slightly rhythmically moving the bottle forward and back.

Sr. Alison also totally banned the dummy, as this would satisfy Anne-Marie's need for sucking, would use up lots of energy, might add to the wind-problem and would tire her out. She encouraged us by saying that she had seen it quite often that after a time of taking very little there could often be a sudden turn-around for the better and so we kept hoping and working toward this oh so elusive improvement.

When Anne-Marie had first come home, I had phoned a number of friends and relations to let them know about the arrival of our little darling. One of these was Johanna Bucher, from near Munich in Germany. On hearing everything about Anne-Marie, including her heart disease, she had quite cheerfully suggested: "Sure, if all fails, you can always come to Munich, to the German Heart Centre there." This was the first time I had heard of its existence. Apparently it was a hospital specializing exclusively in heart problems of both adults and children, which boasted an excellent reputation.

Matthew 11v.25, 26: "At that time Jesus said, "I praise you, Father, Lord of heaven and earth, because you have hidden these things from the wise and learned, and revealed them to little children. Yes, Father, for this was your good pleasure.""

During this time of great feeding problems, Anne-Marie spent most of her time in her buggy as the angled back reduced the vomits and allowed her wind to come up more easily. Sitting on a chair next to Anne-Marie I used to hum or chat to her as a mother might to her baby, never expecting any response of any sort as Anne-Marie was not even eight weeks old. Just to say something positive, and because it was going through my own head one day I said to her "Sure, if all fails, we can always go to Munich, to the German Heart Centre".

Well, I thought I was seeing things. Just as the words had left my mouth, Anne-Marie turned her head round and looked at me with eyes showing full understanding of what I had said, *nodded*, and tried to speak, I am sure in order to confirm that this was a good idea.

This experience electrified me. I wanted to run immediately to arrange a transfer for this so highly unusual child who obviously knew better than I what should happen. I phoned Roland and told him everything that had happened. He was very receptive.

He also said to me that he had been in contact with a consultant friend of his who had had a heart operation when very young. Roland had told his friend how he thought that I had a remarkable attitude towards the possibility of Anne-Marie's death (i.e. 'The Lord giveth, the Lord taketh away, praised be the name of the Lord') only to be told that this attitude was only to be commended if one could be one hundred percent sure that absolutely **_EVERYTHING_** humanly possible had been done to try and save her life. Anne-Marie's strong agreement to going to Munich was certainly an indication to me that we needed to do more to have tried everything humanly possible.

Roland agreed to contact the Heart Centre there and I rang Pat to ask him to get passport application forms for Anne-Marie as we were going to go to Germany. I said I did not know when, but insisted that I was sure we would go, as Anne-Marie herself had indicated it unmistakably. Pat was a little suspicious of the suddenness of this idea but nonetheless quite willing to try to get her passport organised. He is generally not a "spur of the moment" person, preferring instead to let any ideas "mature" before acting on them. He had his hands full running the household, organising the children and holding down his job on a reduced-hours basis without extra jobs like getting passports, but he is a person who never complains.

After the phone call I went back to our little side ward, my thoughts going round and round in excitement. Before long I was called to the phone: Roland. He had been in contact with the German Heart Centre in Munich and spoken to the right man, Dr

Lorenz, explaining Anne-Marie's condition and present situation and enquiring if they would be able to offer her a bed there. Dr. Lorenz was open to the idea of a transfer, saying that he would like Anne-Marie's Belfast cardiologist to contact him and left a fax and telephone number for this purpose.

Roland encouraged me to pursue the transfer. He even informed us what particular E-form we should get for insurance purposes, but both Pat and I were not aware, that this form was difficult to get, and neither of us felt any urgency about getting it.

I spoke to Sr. Alison about the idea of going to Germany. She said she could understand my position, especially with relatives over there who were pushing for the transfer. She advised me to speak to Dr. Craig about it, in order to transfer with full backing from here rather than opting for an under-cover middle-of-the-night-type disappearing act. It was reassuring to feel her openness and support.

While waiting for Dr. Craig's return from his holidays, Anne-Marie started to feed better and better. She was now also getting her full dose of Captopril, and her general condition improved. Therefore, when Dr. Craig finally did come back, I did not mention the subject of the Heart Centre in Munich to him. Instead we were soon discharged home.

Anne-Marie was exceedingly sensitive when we got home. She had got used to our quiet side ward and rejoining the rough-and-tumble household with high-spirited little boys and her toddler-sister who all wanted their mummy came as a bit of a shock and trial to her system. Coughing, shouting, fighting, crying, and the multitude of other loud noises found in our family and home went right through her, making her jerk and shudder.

Even though she seemed adversely affected by all the noise and commotion, she soon developed a nearly insatiable appetite for being involved in or at the very least aware of absolutely everything that was going on around her and would stop feeding to satisfy her curiosity. This meant that I had to keep the kitchen door closed while she was feeding, and poor little Alma experienced being "locked out" like this again and again.

I learned to be gently determined about feeding Anne-Marie, if necessary even against her wishes, and to accept regular vomits as the norm. We recorded each 5ml she took on a sheet of paper attached to the back of the kitchen door, totaling up every 24 hours in order to know Anne-Marie's daily intake. Her top intake was about 90/100mls per meal. At this rate she still needed to be wakened for night feeds but formula milk and the bottle-warmer certainly helped to ease the feeding struggle.

Bit by bit Anne-Marie was filling out and began to have lots of smiles, too. Her personality started to emerge. Our baby had turned into quite a spirited little individual with a lively interest in everything and a tangible sense of humour. She was integrating herself into our family more and more, claiming her rightful place as a full family member. The hospital still kept an eye on her, but they too, were happy with the way things were going. I was settling down to this being the way things were going to be.

Romans 8 v.18: "I consider that our present sufferings are not worth comparing with the glory that will be revealed in us."

Intensive Care

In November 1997 things went wrong. As far as I understand, from the medical point of view, it was not easy to decide what exactly had caused it, but Anne-Marie was described as suffering from heart failure. She had had a different vomit from the norm; usually she would have brought up a barely digested milk vomit. That day it was from further down, with the consistency - if you allow the comparison - of thick boiled porridge.

Having learned to persevere with feeding, even against the odds, I was still quite determined to feed her again, even after this vomit, but she really could not take anything more. After a while I relented and said: "Maybe you're not well?" She looked at me with an expression of love, relief and gratitude, with the slightest hint of a thankful smile. Deep within me I understood.

It was evening time. I phoned Clark Clinic and a nurse advised us to bring Anne-Marie into the hospital in the morning. That night Pat was holding hands with her, reaching across from his bed to her buggy to try to get her over to sleep. She was so restless, breathing fast and grunting with every breath. Pat said she had given him a little loving smile in the middle of all this. A smile, he said, he would never forget.

In the morning all six of us headed off to Clark Clinic. I had Anne-Marie in her car seat on my lap in the front, while Raphael, Pascal and Alma were fighting over the preferred middle seat in the back of the car. Anne-Marie was grunting continually. I heard myself rebuking the backseat passengers: "Imagine you, fighting over the seats, while your little sister here is dying." It was not until the words had left my mouth that I took note of what I had said. Something within me must have been aware of the gravity of Anne-Marie's condition. For the children in the back it was just another trip, one of many, to the hospital.

In order not to disrupt her I wheeled Anne-Marie to Clark Clinic in her car seat on top of the buggy. Dr Casey came towards us in the corridor, took one concerned look at her and said he would be right back. Being in hospital, Anne-Marie was removed from her usual environment and routine. At home she would have gone for her mid-morning nap now, but here too many things were happening. Countless doctors of various grades had to listen to her heart; her blood pressure had to be taken, respirations (or breaths per minute) measured. Going to sleep was impossible for her in these busy surroundings. She was on high mental alert, on overdrive, taking in everything that was going on.

Not to get over-alarmed, she soon needed the extra security of being on my arm. It seemed like every time she had settled enough to maybe drift over to sleep someone came along to do something to her. The one thing that was on nobody's agenda was Anne-Marie's need for sleep. Anne-Marie was getting exhausted on top of being unwell. I felt in my own body how much she needed to be left in peace.

To guard against any possible infection that might have been at the root of this episode it had been decided that Anne-Marie should receive intravenous antibiotics. She was to get a "line" put in her head. I had to agree to this. The doctor arrived just as Anne-Marie was allowing herself to slip into dreamland. He was something of an expert in putting in lines and only needed one attempt to be successful. The doctor had done a marvellous job but now there was no hope of getting Anne-Marie over to sleep. She had had enough. She got into a terrible state.

A combination of medication, illness, stress, pain, emotional turmoil and exhaustion had her beside herself, gasping for air. Sr. Alison brought oxygen. It was well into the afternoon by this stage and there was still no rest or sleep in sight. Holding the tube with the oxygen up to Anne-Marie's face I tried to settle her in the buggy, I tried to settle her on my arm, -without success.

We were moved back into our sideward. Sr. Alison was vigilantly attending to us. Because Anne-Marie had developed a very bad colour, Sr. Alison got her a head-box so that she would have adequate amounts of oxygen. I lay her on her back inside an incubator, and Sr. Alison put a see-through plastic box over her head, into which an oxygen tube was fed. This procedure was very frightening for Anne-Marie but I trusted Sr. Alison.

Even at the time I thanked God that Sr. Alison was there, as knowing me I would probably have felt the need to question this decision should it have come from someone else. It took a very long time before Anne-Marie was calming down a little and looked set to fall into an exhausted sleep. Just then, another doctor came and explained that she had to take some arterial blood to assess the blood gases.

What a torture. Where was the doctor from earlier on, who had had first time success with putting in the line? How could she give any more? Her body pierced repeatedly, she was crying with her last strength mustered from - I do not know where. Yet, the sound of it was pitifully muffled by the head-box and the incubator. The head-box steamed up and the condensation inside prevented her from being able to see me and prevented me also from seeing her.

Her nerves were raw. Any sound, especially the click of the closing incubator-door, made her jerk. The doctors did not seem to be aware of this but Sr. Alison was. She was remarkable. I will never forget how she slid herself between the incubator and the doctors before they might have had a chance to close the little door themselves. She then closed it silently in order to save Anne-Marie (and me) any additional suffering.

A little while later, the same doctor came back saying she would need to take another sample, as the sample she had taken had started to clot by the time she had reached the lab. I felt very cross with her and was starting to let her know this when the utter futility of it struck me, and in an instance my anger melted away leaving me free to enter peacefully into suffering.

Something had changed within me. It came by Grace and with deep Peace. Anne-Marie was suffering beyond measure, but the doctor, too, would have preferred not to have to repeat this torturous procedure. In her own way she was suffering, too. There was no need to add to it by wanting to be cross with her. What could she do now except exactly what she was doing? I had opened up to allowing things to run their course, to letting go of the anxiety caused by wanting to be in control.

Sr. Alison was marvellous at getting across the severity of Anne-Marie's condition to me. It had progressed from "she is not looking well" and "she has a bad colour" to "she is very ill" to "I would say she is the sickest baby on our ward at the moment;" and then from "she may need to go to Intensive Care" to "we are in contact with the Intensive Care Unit to arrange for a transfer."

In the early evening she explained that Anne-Marie was by now so exhausted that were she to go over to sleep she would just stop breathing. In order to prevent this she would need to be on a respirator which would do the breathing for her. That made sense. I asked her if it was difficult to come off such a respirator later. She confirmed that it could be, especially for "heart children".

My only other concern was whether I could be together with Anne-Marie in intensive care. I wanted to be close to her. I felt I had to be an ever-present reminder of her decision to be our/my child, and to try to give her courage to hold out through the hard times, to assure her of being loved and wanted. I felt sure, that if this closeness was disturbed she might just give up and die.

Dr. Casey arrived in the little side-ward with the echo-machine. We were in the dark, watching the screen. He was very calm and gentle. While examining Anne-Marie, her heart rate suddenly jumped up to over 200 beats per minute. He asked for an ice pack and somebody ran to get it. He put it on Anne-Marie's face. The rate dropped back.

Sr. Alison and Dr. Casey advised me to ring Pat, to let him know how serious Anne-Marie's condition was, to tell him that she would have to go to Intensive Care as soon as they were ready for her over there and to ask him to come. I was a little reluctant to leave her side, but they both urged me to ring so I took their advice.

The side-ward was small, and with lockers, incubator and echo scanner inside, it was difficult for me to get out from where I had been. It involved crawling underneath some electric cables, down on my knees. As I crawled out I said that I was saying my prayers. There was no response to my remark. Maybe it had sounded flippant to their ears.

Looking back now, I am a little surprised that I don't remember actually praying during this time. I did not feel abandoned; I did not feel a lack of God's presence. Since the experience of the second arterial blood taking I had become able to allow things to happen without being drawn into wanting to understand or control them. My role was just to be there. Everything else was up to God, to the medics and to Anne-Marie herself.

Pat arrived just as Anne-Marie – fully alert and panting for air in her oxygenated head-box and incubator - was getting transferred to the children's ICU. We were allowed in for only a moment. She was transferred onto a table-like intensive care bed, with a bright light shining down on her and surrounded by a hive of activity which must have been terrifying for her. She held on to my eyes with hers, fearfully clinging, yet reassured that I was there. Then I was sent out.

They were going to insert the tube into her lungs and did not allow me to witness it, saying that I would be in the way. I was sent out at the worst time, at the time of her gravest need. The terror stricken look in her pleading eyes as she saw that I was going to leave her broke my heart.

Romans 8 v.35 & 38: "Who shall separate us from the love of Christ? Shall trouble or hardship or persecution or famine or nakedness or danger or sword? ...I am convinced that neither death nor life, neither angel nor demon neither the present nor the future, nor any powers neither height nor depth nor anything else in all creation will be able to separate us from the love of God that is in Christ Jesus our Lord."

I *understood* that they felt they could work better if I was not there, that they thought I might faint and need attention, and take up what little space there was around her bed. I understood that they would let me back in after about an hour; I understood that they were dedicated to doing everything in their power to save her life, but *having to leave her in her hour of need* was asking too much. Uncontrollable gushes of tears were streaming down my face. There was no end of them in sight. If she were to die now during these procedures she would die among total strangers. The nearest seat to the ICU folding doors was mine and time passed slowly and in streams of tears.

She looked peaceful, so peaceful, when we were allowed back in, breathing evenly - due to the respirator - and sleeping, due to the anaesthetic. Of course, she had a whole host of lines coming out of her - I later counted at least nine - and of course, there was a tube coming out of her nose, but I saw only Anne-Marie. Her little face and whole body looked so relaxed, so calm. She was getting a rest at last.

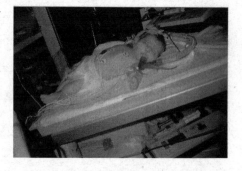

I overheard someone commenting that it had been "touch and go" with her and that she had been got "only just in time." Pat remembers the anesthetist saying that her life had been "on a knife-edge." Thank you, God, for being with her, for providing her with the care she needed, and for giving us strength and support. I was determined not to leave her side once allowed back in. I had decided to spend the night by her side.

Day by day I grew a little more accepting of the fact that I needed my own sleep, too. Thankfully, I never had any problems with getting to sleep. Just as soon as my head hit the pillows I was away. I felt very privileged to be allowed to sleep in a room directly across the corridor from the ICU. During the daytime this was one of two parent rooms, to be used by all the parents and families of the children in the ICU, and at night-time it was kindly turned into my sleeping quarters. I was also offered the use of the parent flat provided by the "Heartbeat"[8] charity. It was a short walk away, but I wanted to be close.

The ICU night staff agreed to call me as soon as they were going to do any work with Anne-Marie so that I could be there when she was awake. Initially, it depended very much upon the staff on duty how seriously they took this arrangement but after a few *painful* upsets it worked very well.

My sister Verena, phoning from Germany, encouraged me again and again to stand by my requests, even in the face of opposition. This sometimes took energy that I was not sure I had. She would say: "I am right behind you, remember this, when you are speaking with them," and it really made a tremendous difference.

Sr. Alison, too, looked in on a regular basis, giving me moral support and helping me not to allow Anne-Marie's care to slip out of my hands altogether. She was *invaluably* encouraging and practical, answering any questions honestly and highlighting ways of doing things. With her support I was allowed to tube feed Anne-Marie when she came off intravenous feeds and to see to her personal care, such as nappy changes and cleaning around her mouth and eyes as well as bed baths.

A common reason for a nighttime knock on my door was "suction." This involved a very unpleasant procedure of inserting a plastic tube into Anne-Marie's nose and upper respiratory passages. It worked a little like a vacuum cleaner, sucking up any loose mucus, and necessitated her being temporarily disconnected from the respirator. On occasions this left her gasping for breath. It was a distressing practice for her and often considerably raised her heart rate, sometimes to dangerously high levels. But with all the tubes stuck in her throat all her crying was silent.

There were also occasions when her heart rate would spontaneously jump to over 200 beats per minute. Quick ice-bag reactions helped initially, but later she needed rapidly administered intravenous injections to bring the rate down again. Her heart would not have been able to continue pumping at such a fast rate for long. A maximum of three of these injections were allowed on any one occasion, with a prescribed time elapsing between them. And even though initially she would respond to the first injection, and later she sometimes needed the second, there was never a time when she did not respond to the third. - Thanks be to God.

Eventually I was also allowed to stay with her during her numerous x-rays so long as I wore the appropriate protective jacket. Other treatments included physiotherapy, during which her little chest was rhythmically pushed down while she was lying on her side or back. This was necessary in order to prevent her lungs from getting too congested, and/or from collapsing; or in order to try to help certain collapsed areas to recover. It was very strenuous for her to get 'physio' when she was at her weakest and on one occasion she turned a ghastly green colour afterwards.

I wanted to be with Anne-Marie to support her in her time of need, to be a reminder to her that she had chosen to come to us and to encourage her to hold out. I tried as much as possible to speak to her in a soothing way and to maintain eye contact with her to prevent her from feeling bewildered and abandoned during these procedures. Of course I also helped to hold her in position when this was needed. Some of the medical and paramedical staff were encouraging and maybe even encouraged by my wanting to be close while others reacted considerably less favourably.

Most of the time, when she was awake, Anne-Marie's eyes were alert and showing full awareness. One of the doctors remarked half-jokingly that she did not like to work with Anne-Marie, as she always looked her straight in the eyes whenever she was about to do something to her.

1 John 4 v. 18: "There is no fear in love. But perfect love drives out fear."

Dr Craig was something of an oasis to a worried and concerned mother, always answering any questions patiently with great professionalism and compassion. I had plenty of time to marvel at his ability to be so professional and so humane and caring under such pressure as was his, taking responsibility for the very lives of the children in his care on his shoulders with every decision he made.

I realised that had he been afraid of making wrong decisions this would have inhibited his work. What shone through his way of working was God's great love. I felt certain (without ever speaking about it to him) that it was just *this*, God's love, which kept him going and going and going. It was *this*, which gave him such compassion and the desire to do everything possible to help. It was tangibly a case of 'perfect love casts out all fear.'

An ICU information sheet made Pat and me aware that there was a hospital chaplain who could be contacted via the named nurse. Jane made an appointment for him to come and pray a blessing on Anne-Marie. Somewhere along the line the message must have been a little distorted because he arrived expecting to baptise Anne-Marie. This was fine with Pat and me, so long as we were not baptising repeatedly. I mentioned Anne-Marie's baptismal history to the chaplain and he then suggested that he could use a turn of phrase like: "In as far as you have not already been baptised, I baptise you now..." This seemed good to us and it would make her baptism official.

Anne-Marie was fast asleep. It was a sedation-induced deep sleep. To all intents and purposes Anne-Marie was totally oblivious to all that was happening around her – her eyes closed, and her body asleep. Unperturbed by this, the little ceremony went ahead. Everything was normal enough until suddenly, when the words "*I baptise you in the name of the Father, the Son, and the Holy Spirit*" were pronounced over her, to our total amazement, Anne-Marie opened her eyes and looked straight into the Chaplain's eyes. As soon as the words had been spoken she closed her eyes and did not open them again during the rest of the little ceremony. We all thought this highly unusual and very striking. Anne-Marie had consciously received the Sacrament and again broken through physical norms by her extraordinary response to it.

During a ward round or a new admission or when a death had occurred parents were not allowed into the ICU. The reason for sending parents out during ward rounds was unclear to me. Wanting to be integrated as fully as possible into Anne-Marie's care I thought of access to her medical information as something of a natural right. This might have had something to do with the fact that before I had become a mother I used to read and write into medical notes on a professional basis.

Ultimately, though, I think it was less the need to be up to date with her medical condition than the sense of being sorely needed by Anne-Marie which motivated me to question the regulations. I had found on a number of occasions that if I was not with her for an hour or more while she lay awake, her eyes would look duller, more distant and less responsive when I was finally allowed back in. I talked to a nurse about this at the door of the ICU while the ward round was in progress. She tried to reassure me that all of Anne-Marie's medical needs were being seen to, even during the ward-round.

I explained that I did not doubt what she said, but that Anne-Marie's other needs, such as her social and spiritual ones, needed to be accommodated too, as far as possible under the circumstances, to facilitate her well being. I described Anne-Marie's eyes and their detached gaze of distant dullness if I was absent from her for too long while she was awake and mentioned that I was also interested in hearing what the doctors had to say about her condition. After the staff had considered my concerns I was allowed to be present during the ward round whenever Anne-Marie was being discussed. I was very thankful for the flexible approach of the unit.

When I remembered the relationship between Anne-Marie and the icon of St. John the Baptist, which was still hanging in our living room at home, I thought Anne-Marie might be further encouraged to hold out if she was close to it again. I asked Pat to bring it in and was granted permission to fasten it behind the head-end of Anne-Marie's bed. It was reassuring to see John the Baptist watching over everything.

I spent my days sitting by her side, humming and talking to her. I made a point of reading or quietly chanting prayers from an Orthodox prayer book to her. During the nights I continued rushing to be at her side every time someone was working with her. Of course I was losing out on quite a bit of sleep which was difficult to make up again, as the parent room was open to all during the day and "my" bed turned back into a settee, but to me it was worth everything to be with my little darling during her hard times.

In retrospect I feel that this arrangement helped me to be at peace later on, at the time of Anne-Marie's death. I did not have to wrestle with feelings of guilt, of not having done enough for her, which I believe can so easily tear at one's heart at a time of loss. We lived through her difficulties together, side-by-side, and I thank God for that. It would have been far harder to be separated, not having enough time to keep up a meaningful relationship, and never knowing how she was.

The ICU was a demanding setting. Two children died while Anne-Marie was in the ICU, one after a struggle of many weeks and the other after a very short and sudden illness. And although in all cases the medical staff kept everything strictly confidential the parent rooms were filled with immeasurable pain and anguish. Details of the children's conditions were gone over and over again and again, in an effort to come to grips with them; in an effort to begin to understand what was happening and why, hardly daring to look at what might or might not happen later on.

I got to know one of Jade's grannies. Jade was a little girl who had lost her whole immediate family in a house fire. Granny was still under so much shock that she had not been able to cry yet, numb after having laid her son and daughter-in-law and two grandchildren to rest. She just functioned, waiting for everything to hit her. She showed me family photographs she carried with her in her handbag.

Another child, a little boy, had just regained some level of consciousness after being very critically ill with a head injury. He had been in his childminder's car when it was hit by a recklessly driven lorry.

The knife-edge experience of life and death of beloved babies, toddlers and schoolchildren required great strength. Everyone had to find his or her own responses. Some had to take frequent breaks from seeing their little ones so critically ill, others found it harder to be away from them. People were praying earnestly. It was good to hear someone say "I'll pray for her" and to know that, yes, they definitely would because they knew the score so well themselves.

1 Kings 19 v.4-8: " … an angel touched him and said, "Get up and eat." He looked around, and there by his head was a cake of bread baked over hot coals, and a jar of water. He ate and drank and then lay down again. The angel of the Lord came back a second time and touched him and said, "Get up and eat, for the journey is too much for you." So he got up and ate and drank. Strengthened by that food, he travelled for forty days and forty nights until he reached Horeb, the mountain of God."

Initially, the whole ICU situation affected my appetite. Any food I ate just tasted like cardboard, and for a while I felt an aversion against eating. Then, one day, thankfully still towards the beginning of the intensive care time, I became vividly aware of the Old Testament quote: *"Get up and eat, or the journey will be too long for you."* It resounded within me for my own desert situation and convinced me that I, too, had to eat and drink even if the food did taste like cardboard.

One morning around five or six o'clock after having been in attendance for some procedure I was still sitting by Anne-Marie's side after she had just gone back to sleep. Although tired, I was filled with peace and love and did not want to rush off to lie down again. I liked to look at her and to just *be with her.*

Dr. Taylor, one of the main ICU Anaesthetist-Consultants, probably sensing the silent beauty of the moment, drew up quietly to stand with us. He had come to speak to me gently, to remind me to look after myself, too. He said: "Which ever way this is going to go, you will need your strength to get through the time that lies ahead." I felt genuine concern in what he said. He also pointed out that it could go on like this for quite some time. I nodded in agreement and said, "It's a long way through the desert."

Quietly confiding in him, I entrusted to him my observation that being with Anne-Marie actually *gave* me energy rather than draining it from me and I recounted how Anne-Marie and I had had many silent conversations.

As I said this, I was aware of the gaze of St. John the

Baptist looking peacefully and lovingly at us from the icon, his hands held so as to receive and carry any burdens he might be given. It was as if he was blessing us with his presence. The truth of what I had said stayed with me. It was indeed possible for Anne-Marie and me to have silent conversations just by looking into each other's eyes. She could convey her whole being in and through her eyes.

Medically speaking, the initial aim was to stabilise her. Bit by bit the number of lines and drips was getting smaller. Once she would be stable enough and able to absorb her feeds again, she might be able to come off the respirator and thus start to make her way out of intensive care.

The decision to remove her respirator tube came maybe not at an ideal time, as she was running a little temperature, but I was told that sometimes the tubes can foster infections and Anne-Marie would be better off without it if she could manage.

Anne-Marie was in a terrible state, gasping for air. Hoping that she would be able to get used to breathing by herself again, I held her on my arm to try to settle her and to calm her down. I was standing up with her, holding her upright, her belly against my chest. I was moving up and down from my knees and/or rocking her from side to side while humming or speaking softly and quietly to her, - all to no avail. Sweat was breaking out all over me as I tried my best to hold and rock her, hum, and walk as far as all the tubes allowed, all at the same time.

Dr Taylor and another doctor stood at a respectful distance observing her, and after a good while of no success, they came to tell me that she needed to be intubated again as she was not able to cope without the help of the respirator. Inwardly I was hugely disappointed about this and all that entailed (i.e., general anaesthetic to put the tube back in, etc.). She was intubated again, and when I was allowed back in, she was on all clean sheets, but there was still a drop of fresh blood on the floor.

Slowly the aims were changing, and eventually Dr Craig explained, that it was becoming clear that when stable enough Anne-Marie would need an operation as she was unable to cope with her heart the way it was.

One day I was feeling particularly low. During a time when I was not allowed to visit, I was sitting in the parent room feeling quite hopeless. I had been told that Anne-Marie's kidneys were beginning to give trouble and whoever had told me this had not said it with a hopeful face. This was the first time I had a momentary glimpse of the crushing and paralysing sense of defeat, of hopelessness and helplessness, a glimpse of the grief a mother must feel when she can do nothing except to watch her child die. It was the first time that I felt an abyss of black despair opening up in front of me.

I decided to give Pat a ring from the payphone in the parent room. I lifted the receiver and, as expected, heard the dialing tone, put the money in, rang our number and waited. The phone at our house was ringing but no one answered it. Waiting for someone to lift the phone at home, I heard a singing voice on the line while the ringing tones continued in the foreground. I thought this unusual but did not pay too much attention to it and hung-up the phone when I was sure that no one was going to answer.

Once I had put the phone down, just out of curiosity, I checked if the singing voice was still audible if I lifted the receiver again. But there was only a straightforward dialing tone. I was not surprised, although very slightly disappointed, and then decided to ring Anne-Marie's godparents.

After dialing their number there was the ringing signal again, and to my surprise, there was the same voice as before singing in the background. This time I decided not to hang up if there was no answer but to listen to the singing instead. It was more beautiful than I could put into words. A clear and open angelic voice was freely singing out a most intriguing series of notes and melodies, on occasions dropping into, and winding its way through a stretch of mournful minor notes of Middle Eastern flavour but also finding its way back to brighter and more hopeful notes. These were melodies which I have since found mirrored in some of the Orthodox chants.

I was totally transfixed, listening and absorbing every note with my whole being. It was dissolving my anguish. I was forgetting my troubles. I was being ministered to, even though I did not immediately realise this. The last twelve notes left a sense of excitement with me. I was sure that I knew this melody from somewhere. The singing finished with these notes:

Then there was silence, a very noticeable silence behind the ringing tone of the phone, which nobody was going to lift.

I hung up and marvelled about what had happened to me. I was filled with wonder and awe. My sense of gloom had gone. Now there was hope and new energy. I was captivated by those last notes and spent around two hours wondering about this melody until, sitting by Anne-Marie's side, I finally remembered the words I had sung with those notes in the past:

"...and all that is within me praise His holy name."

I was filled with joy and hope and great excitement in the middle of the bleak intensive care situation with my little daughter beside me so severely ill. I felt reassured that God was with us, I felt I had been ministered to and refreshed by the singing of an angel.

John 17 v. 21: "...that all of them may be one, Father, just as you are in me and I am in you. May they also be in us so that the world may believe that you have sent me."

Many people were praying for us. Family and friends, locally and around the world; Christians of all sorts of backgrounds - Orthodox, Protestant, Catholic, were united in prayer to God for Anne-Marie. The Lamb of God Community, the new Lutheran pastor in Dublin, the Focolare Movement as well as prayer partners of Brother Jardine's "Interdenominational Divine Healing Ministries" at St Anne's Cathedral, Belfast were interceding for us and all helped to suspend us in a net of prayer which lifted us out of reach of the fangs of the fierce and prowling enemy.

I myself could not pray for anything specific, regarding Anne-Marie. I was unable to ask God to heal her. Especially since the experience on the telephone, the praise of God was the only prayer I could pray. The words of the hymn had become my direction. I praised Him for his perfect ways and plans, so far removed from our human understanding. I didn't even *want* to ask for anything, believing instead that the Lord already knew what was needed much better than I, and that He would provide everything at the right time.

Every time I had dark thoughts, I had only to sing praises to God in my heart or to softly sing them to Anne-Marie, and *invariably* my troubles dwindled, my darkness disappeared, and my strength was restored. It was remarkable to experience this over and over again.

I used to particularly sing:

> *Praise the Lord, O my soul*
> *Praise the Lord, O my soul*
> *And all that is within me*
> *Praise His Holy name.*

My meditation on you
Shall be sweet, I shall give praise
To the Lord, while I have my being.
My meditation on you shall be sweet,
I shall give praise to the Lord all my days.
Praise you the Lord, O my soul, praise you the Lord,
Praise you the Lord, O my soul, praise you the Lord,
Praise you the Lord, O my soul, praise you the Lord,
Praise you the Lord, O my soul, praise you the Lord.

It became "Anne-Marie's song." It became my staff on our journey through the desert, through the valley of the shadow of death, my light in the darkness and my well of fresh water in the middle of the desert drought. So, with the help of all the prayers and praise, I usually coped surprisingly well. The visitors testified to this, remarking how amazed they were to see me so strong.

I do, however, remember one particular incident which caught me unawares. 'Would I mind if the side of Anne-Marie's head was shaved in order to add another line?' It seemed strange to me to be given a say in this detail. Would her hair not grow back again? The thought that she would look a less attractive corpse with the side of her head shaven was the only reason I could find for this inquiry.

I opted for keeping her tufts of hair and when they were given to me in a little cellophane bag it seemed a real possibility that these little bits of hair could be the only thing I would be left holding. I just could not help the tears running down my face, even in front of the doctors and nurses. I was overcome by grief.

My cousin Roland, having worked in paediatric intensive care himself, wanted to be informed about everything that was happening to Anne-Marie. And even though initially Anne-Marie was hardly fit to be turned over on her bed, let alone to be transported to Germany, he kept mentioning a transfer to Munich.

Roland greatly appreciated the ICU team's dedication to save Anne-Marie's life. He was impressed by all their efforts. His comment: "They are fighting like lions for her" still rings in my ear. Certainly everyone had done their best for Anne-Marie but eventually there was not a lot more they could do.

The situation came to a head. Dr. Craig, Sr. Alison and a member of the ICU team called me into the parent room for a meeting. I felt outnumbered, but their warmth and concern were reassuring. Decisions had to be made. Up to now I had not had to sign any consent forms regarding Anne-Marie but now that she was regarded as "stable" in ICU terms her future had to be mapped out.

Anne-Marie was assessed as not being able to breathe independently. She needed the respirator to help her breathe. Of course, that situation could not be allowed to continue indefinitely as prolonged artificial respiration has its own risks. The conclusion that was drawn - to be approved by me – was, that pending the final decision by the cardiac surgeon, we would opt for an operation.

The cardiac surgeon had already had a look at the notes

and found some inconsistency in the pressures inside Anne-Marie's heart as determined by the echo scans. In order to have a better knowledge of the actual pressures in her heart he had recommended explorative catheterisation. This, to my understanding, involved gaining access to the heart by sliding a catheter into it via one of the blood vessels. I was to give my permission for this. It was to happen on Monday. I said "yes, yes."

I understood the plan. I agreed with it, rationally, but I had a sense of doom. Everything seemed unreal. Whether Dr Craig noticed this, or whether he would customarily ask a second time I do not know, but I was grateful for his enquiring again if I was *sure* as I would have to sign the consent form on Monday and even catheterization involved a certain amount of risk.

As he put it like this I requested to be allowed to sleep on it and to discuss it with my husband. That seemed reasonable to all concerned and they left me. I felt as though somebody had punched me in the stomach. I was winded. Even though my head could fully understand the position, it seemed to leave the rest of me behind. My heart was not committed to what my head had approved of.

Isaiah 41 v.16 "... along unfamiliar paths I will guide them; I will turn the darkness into light before them and make the rough places smooth."

Roland was one of the first to hear about the new plans. He fervently urged me to push for a move to Munich. I was reluctant to ask for a transfer as I felt that this might give staff in Belfast the erroneous impression that I was not satisfied with the treatment offered here. Yet Anne-Marie's own approval of going to Munich was very much alive in my mind, while the continually pleading voice of his consultant-friend to try *everything* humanly possible was not allowing Roland to be satisfied with anything less.

He argued that it is better to go to a hospital with an internationally established good reputation like Munich than to an internationally largely unknown entity like Belfast. And although I realised that if she were to be operated here and things went wrong, I would never be able to say that I had done all I could, there was still a reluctance to ask about a transfer. I did not want to seem ungrateful.

Roland sensed my hesitation and pushed me onwards, saying, "What is a person's pride in comparison with the life of your child?" The word "pride" was wholly unsuitable for such a genuine gentleman as Dr Craig but I understood. It was my own pride I had to overcome, my own pride of wanting to be seen as an appreciative sort of person. It had to be abandoned.

At the very next opportunity I approached Dr Craig. To my great relief he was open to the idea of a transfer to Munich. Children in a stable condition like Anne-Marie had been transferred by air ambulance to Birmingham, and in principle there was no reason why this should not be done to Munich. He pointed out that it depended on a number of organisational arrangements and especially also on an agreement on the part of Munich to take her. Moreover he added thoughtfully that it would be a very costly undertaking.

Roland's complete commitment flashed through my mind. On one occasion he had insisted that cost was absolutely not to be a hindrance to any of our plans and that if the worst came to the worst he would sell a piece of land he had, he would sell his grand piano, he would sell his car and, if it took more than that, more would be found.

Dr Craig was satisfied to hear this and enquired if I wanted the catheter study to be done in Belfast or in Munich. I opted for everything to be carried out in Germany, thinking that they might like to do their own assessments and that their conclusions might be different from those arrived at here and that the risk attached to catheterisation could jeopardise the transfer plans.

Dr Craig made contact with Munich and very reassuringly described Dr Lorenz, the consultant cardiologist of the paediatric intensive care unit in the German Heart Centre there, as a very nice man, and reported that he was willing to take Anne-Marie as a patient.

Roland made enquiries into the German air ambulance services even though we had gone ahead and booked a British one. In a British air ambulance a senior anesthetist and a nurse, who already knew Anne-Marie would travel with her, and Anne-Marie's present respirator would be compatible with the one on the airplane. The hand-over would be at the Munich Hospital. Dr

Craig was not sure if there would also be a seat for me on the plane. I simply trusted that there would be.

Pat tried to obtain the correct form for covering medical costs within Europe for dependants of someone employed and still living in the UK, but it was not just a matter of picking up the form. It had to be applied for. Nobody could say if we were actually going to get it but as a concession they gave him a script which said that our application was presently being considered. Anne-Marie's passport had already been organized.

More details emerged. The British air ambulance was to cost around £10,000. Return journeys for the Belfast staff would have to be arranged and I would have to make my own independent travel arrangements to the German Heart Centre. I found the idea of leaving Anne-Marie alone for the duration of the journey nearly intolerable. I feared that she would die en route if I was not with her. But Dr. Craig had made it clear that that was how it would be and I was left to chew on it.

Roland in the meantime established that the German air ambulance price was far lower, and that they *were able to take me* as well. They had made a very good impression on him and he urged me to take them if I was giving any credence to the German health system at all. He reasoned that they had their own on-board doctors who were accustomed to the medical equipment on board.

The British air ambulance had been booked. It was the weekend and Dr. Craig was not on duty. I was reluctant to disturb him at home. Roland urged me. *My* main motivating factor was that I would be allowed on board, too. There was going to be a senior anesthetist as well as a nurse-technician (in one person) present, which would leave one seat for an extra passenger: myself. I had to try.

Dr Craig was a little surprised. He was also anxious to ensure that Anne-Marie would receive comprehensive care during the flight and that there would be a proper hand-over procedure at the hospital where the compatibility of equipment would need to be thoroughly verified. He was warning against a quick and possibly slipshod transfer at the airport.

We explored different variables and finally settled for the German air ambulance with their own staff on board the flight. I agreed to arrange the hand-over at the Belfast hospital and Dr Craig was going to cancel the British services. The date for the journey was to be Tuesday, 25 November 1997.

Our neighbour Sharon had collected a contribution from the people of our street and a friend brought a generous donation including German currency and a card from her colleague, also with money. I was humbled. It was touching to see how people cared so much. Of course, apart from the big expense of any operation and hospital stay there was the flight, the cost of the ambulance from Munich airport to the hospital and my living expenses in Munich, which all had to be seen to. Yet, supported by sustained intercessory prayer I felt confident that God was in charge and that things were going His way.

It was an afterthought on my part to remember that I would have to bed down somewhere in Munich, too. I had been assuming that these things would sort themselves out. I rang and enquired if I could sleep in the hospital during Anne-Marie's stay there. A male nurse told me that I could probably stay in the parents' quarters. I asked him to let them know that I was coming on Tuesday, 25 November, and he said he would.

The day of departure came. An ambulance went out to the City Airport to collect the doctor and nurse/technician together with their incubator and equipment for hand-over at the Belfast hospital. I had been warned to keep luggage to an absolute minimum. The icon of St. John the Baptist was part of that absolute minimum. I went to the bathroom one last time in the ICU parent rooms. Another mother commented when I came out that I must be very happy that we were leaving; I hadn't even noticed that I had been singing in the bathroom!

Anne-Marie was transferred into the German incubator with temperature regulation and breathing apparatus. Heavy sedation had to be given so that she would not breathe against the machinery she was going to be attached to. Unlike the respirator she had been used to, with the German one she could not initiate the breaths or breathe in a percentage of the air herself.

Alert to the unusual circumstances, Anne-Marie refused to respond to the sedation properly. Only half way to the airport the doctor reported that she had finally stopped fighting against the machines and that the sedation was working properly. To me it was saying only now was she relaxing and giving herself into the flow of events

The ambulance driver, John, had been the one who had taken Anne-Marie from the Mater Hospital to the Royal Neonatal Intensive Care Unit on the day of her birth. I thanked him again for his part in saving her life. He told us how he had had the blue lights flashing and the sirens on all the way from the Mater to the Royal that time. I had not known this and hearing it gave me a grateful pang.

It gave me another glimpse of how desperately ill Anne-Marie had been even then. It gave me love in my heart for the matter-of-fact emergency work John was doing by being a children's emergency ambulance driver. It also gave me a glimpse of how important Anne-Marie was - and we all are: well established traffic regulations had been overruled by her need to get into Intensive Care. All the people on their busy and important missions in their cars had to come second to the little baby girl on her way to hospital.

It was a grey and windy day. There might even have been a skift of rain in it. A small plane was waiting for us. The ambulance was allowed onto the airfield without any checks. I thanked John and he wished us all the very best. With his eyes and with his handshake he wished us every good thing now that we were leaving to where he could not be of service.

2 Corinthians 12 v. 8: "My grace is sufficient for you for my power is made perfect in weakness."

Munich

The men carried the incubator with its precious load and any pieces of equipment into the little fast-looking jet. There was hardly enough room to stand upright. I got on with my bag and icon. My bag was put in the back of the plane and I kept the icon in its hospital bag in my very limited foot space, which meant that my feet had to be at an awkward angle for the duration of the flight, but I was grateful to have got this far.

It was a fast and noisy flight. The doctor wanted to know why we were not taking Anne-Marie to London. He had heard of a number of German children who had been taken there for their heart operations. He also mentioned Berlin but granted that Munich was probably as good as London or Berlin.

Again and again my eyes read over a big German notice on the wall directly in front of me. I became aware of the curious way in which all nouns begin with a capital letter. Of course, having grown up in Germany this was nothing really new to me. But what *was* new was the Realisation that the very Fact of spelling Nouns this Way was a Reflection of the German Mentality. In no other Language I had heard of were Things honoured in the same Way.

This was the place we were heading for. This was the place I had escaped from, to Ireland, where material things still largely had to take a backseat behind human values, and where the churches fill up (noticeably on Sundays) with people looking for spiritual food. I had to get prepared, inwardly, for Germany.

Anne-Marie was and is a real means of reconciliation. I had to acknowledge that the German values of precision and quality were not to be belittled. After all, I was placing Anne-Marie into their hands. The challenge would be to marry the Irish profound (faith-based) concern and love for people to the German efficiency without compromising on either.

We were speeding along the light blue sky. The doctor directed me to the on-board supply of snacks and drinks but I felt more loyal to Pat's variety of cardboard. I felt an already indebted guest and was reluctant to further exacerbate the situation. Of course, this was highly irrational as thousands of pounds were going to change hands for the flight and a sandwich or two would not have made any difference. I changed my mind after a while and filled my pocket in view of uncertain food supplies to come.

We landed in Munich. A fluorescent red-coloured ambulance was on standby and as soon as our plane had come to a standstill it drew up, parking at a little distance from our jet. Being in the front seat I had to get out first. I went over towards the ambulance. Out of it emerged a tall and lean figure with a flowing extra-crisp white coat and silver grey hair: Dr. Peters.

In a very friendly and forthcoming manner he ushered me into the front passenger seat of the ambulance, and with his somewhat backward-bouncing gait hurried over to the plane. This was it. First taste of parenthood German-style: "You sit here while we look after your child." In Belfast I had sat by Anne-Marie in the back of the ambulance, here now I was to be in the front, so to speak in the cabin, completely separated but for a small window through which one could see little of what was happening in the main part.

I got out again to join the doctors in their hand-over. They emerged, running with baby wrapped in white blanket flapping in the wind into the back of the ambulance. Anne-Marie was put in the hospital's incubator and attached to all their machinery in the ambulance.

On arrival at Munich Heart Centre – Deutsches Herzzentrum München - my Anne-Marie was wheeled away in her incubator plus equipment. I was intent on not being ushered away this time. I grabbed my luggage and hurried in after them through a confusing array of very large automated glass doors. I had lost them for an instant, but -oh good, there they still were. I rushed to catch up before they might disappear again, travel bag, handbag, icon in hand, only to be told that I had to go to the hospital administration first to book Anne-Marie in. This was *always* the first thing to be done and, sure, I could come up to the ward to see her afterwards.

Away she disappeared into a lift and I ended up trying to explain to two very nice and compassionate administration ladies how it could be that we had arrived, doctor on board of ambulance, without anyone in administration knowing anything about this admission and how, furthermore, it could be that Anne-Marie was already on the ward, but that - nearly incomprehensibly - the whole thing had happened without there being any written evidence whatsoever as to who was going to pay for all of this! We were all scratching our heads in unison.

Finally I produced a letter from somebody in Stormont (local government building in Belfast) stating that they were in the process of deciding whether or not they might issue the appropriate E-number form for us. Thankfully the administration ladies were delighted with this script, photocopying it there and then, and phoning up their superior about it, who also seemed to be more appeased at being able to put an official script onto the file.

There I was, out of administration, bags in hand, wanting nothing except to be with Anne-Marie. I got the lift up to the children's intensive care ward. I had reached the ward, but not yet Anne-Marie, when a nurse confronted me and said that there had been a little confusion as to my arrival as I had not rung a second time to reconfirm arrangements for a parent room.

She emphasized that I was very lucky because they had just had a phone call from McDonald House[9] informing her of an unexpected vacancy. I was urged to go over *immediately* as they could not keep the room for me if I did not take it within the next 20 minutes. I was assured it was not very far and that I could see

Anne-Marie afterwards. Of course, I tried to say that I wanted to stay with Anne-Marie and go to the parents' house later. I was granted a quick look at her - still sleeping - and then ushered along, quickly, quickly, so that my room would not be given to someone else. What could I do? I set off for McDonald House.

Out of the hospital, turn right, and along the road. Find some tall black gates. Hurrying along my bag got heavier and I was sweating in my thick red woolly jumper and my old blue raincoat. I found the gate. It was locked. I tried it a number of times, but it was definitely locked. I looked around for a bell or maybe an intercom but found none. I was too much in a hurry to be held up by a silly locked gate too high to climb over. I stuck my hand through a gap between the bars and tried the handle on the inside of the gate - success. Along the path, there it was: McDonald house – locked; I rang the bell and read the notice on the door. One was supposed to take off one's outdoor-shoes on entering. We have definitely arrived in Germany, the well-organised Place of Rules and Regulations.

I was invited into the office. First things first. A friendly lady took my details and my deposit (thank you RoseAnne for your present of correct currency) and explained the rules of the house of which there were quite a few…the cleaning rota, the kitchen facilities, the price of staying, of phone calls, etc., She then gave me a folder with important local information and the key to my room, number 4.

She stressed how incredibly lucky I was, to arrive and virtually walk in and get a room. Usually people had to take a room in a more or less local guesthouse or hotel first and then wait for a vacancy. Had I come an hour earlier, the previous occupants would still have been there and I would have been sent away. To the surprise of the McDonald House management they had left suddenly, just before my arrival. Had I not come now the next person walking in would have got the room as they were given out on a first-come, first-served basis. I told the lady in the office that I had no doubt that My Lord had arranged the accommodation for me. This sort of fine-tuning bore His signature to me, and she didn't disagree. My heart was encouraged to sense the presence of God and inwardly I sang His praises.

She showed me the room: En-suite with shower cubicle and toilet. There were two single pine beds and a big window. (I also seem to remember a glass door to a balcony.) She explained something about having only just hung the freshly washed over-curtains. It was irrelevant to me.

The room was clean, airy and spacious, with lots of storage facilities and with fresh bed linen folded on top of lovely light duvets. There was a telephone on the bedside table and two framed scenery photographs on the wall. Everything was perfect: too perfect. I grew ungrateful. I did not *want* to be in a beautiful room five or more minutes' walk away from Anne-Marie! I wanted to be with Anne-Marie, room or no room, bed or no bed. The pine beds smelled of money to me, of unwanted comfort and luxury. I did not want to partake of it, it was repulsive to me. How could I enjoy this while Anne-Marie was lying somewhere else unable to even move her head, fixed as it was into one position by the tubes of the respirator coming out of her nose? Yet I knew God had been gracious in providing the room for me. Without it I would have ended up further away and paying more.

And I *was* grateful - grateful that I could finally leave my bag behind and hurry out, round along the street back into the big spacious modern marble-floored hospital. Under normal conditions I would probably have appreciated or simply not noticed the architecture of it but on this day the whole building oozed out an air of uncalled-for grandeur and intimidation. It was a place that made me feel insignificant, lost and alien. This imposing hospital was a daunting physical barrier between Anne-Marie and me who were somehow both put in place - a place of inferiority and dependence upon automated doors and equipment which threatened to swallow up our humanity. During my first few days there this building caused anger to well up inside me.

The old Royal Victoria Hospital for Sick Children had been a homely place, full of people helping each other without any airs of anything other than that. The people of *this* institution seemed to be actively supporting an alien framework of unnecessary physical barriers. These thoughts and feelings were involuntarily shaping my perception of their attitude toward parents as a superfluous and unwelcome hindrance to their work.

It was uncomfortably noticeable, too, that no one seemed willing to enter into any general conversations or to be forthcoming with any low-key chat about themselves (or about the weather!). This applied to all levels of staff –the cleaners, 'Zivis'[10], nurses, paramedics and doctors. Everyone was too professional to consider human contact or anything beyond their immediate duty as important. At the same time no one was scheduled to give an account to the parents of what was happening.

The Children's Intensive Care Unit was on the third floor. There was an intercom speaker with a button fixed to the wall beside the visitors' locked entry door. After pressing the button one had to hope for some merciful person to answer the call at the other end of the ward. This could sometimes take more than ten minutes. There was no provision for sitting down anywhere even though some of the mothers had only recently given birth and were looking pale and weak.

Once the disembodied voice had verified your entitlement to come in and then activated a snib-opening device from the other end of the ward, the first stage was accomplished. In the changing room you were supposed to hang up your coat and bag, put on a sterile gown and disinfect your hands. That was fine. The door from there into the ward was locked shut and opened only if the lever of a dispenser of disinfectant fixed onto the wall at the right side of this door was pressed.

A skilled person would press this lever with their left hand having the right hand ready to receive the liquid out of the dispenser while the door clicked open and would then pull the door open with the left hand, wide enough to slide a foot in to the gap, while rubbing the liquid on both hands before entering the ward.

An unskilled person might stand by the door, press the lever, receive the liquid, disinfect their hands and then try to pull the door open, which at that stage, more often than not, would be securely locked again. I also met someone in this area who had not been able to work out how to open this door, and had thus been trapped in the changing room.

Having got out of the "Schleuse" (lock) was by no means equivalent to being allowed to see your child. Depending on what the voice at the first door had said, one might very well be only allowed to proceed to the back of the ward where there *were* some chairs and to wait there until called to proceed onwards to the particular section one's child was in.

When I finally got to Anne-Marie, without asking anyone, I fixed the icon of St. John the Baptist onto the inside of her ICU cot behind her head. The icon fitted in beautifully and had a peace-giving effect on me. Long-suffering, unquestioned acceptance, the assurance of his unshakeable protective role radiated out through the icon across the little bed where Anne-Marie lay sleeping. I had to give her into God's hands.

Staff came to tell me to go – visiting time had ended. I do not know how long I had been there, but I certainly did not feel ready to go. How would she feel when she wakened and mummy was nowhere to be seen? Would anyone rush to attend to her if she was trying to cough? She could not make herself heard, of course. With the pipes in her throat, her voice box had no chance. Would she get physiotherapy to clear the left upper section of her lungs on which there had been a shadow before leaving from Belfast?

In Belfast, the main ICU ward - where nearly all the patients were - was never left unattended. If suction was required it was immediately available. Here I felt on the sidelines. The ward was divided into numerous side wards with, as far as I could see, one, two or three ICU beds to each sideward. There could not be a nurse to every side ward and consequently for some periods of time there were no members of staff at all in some of these side wards.

I felt Anne-Marie's breathing was "rattly" and it took me what seemed to be an eternity before I was able to alert staff to this. The nurse I spoke to was neither thankful nor happy about my telling her and did not act on my observation. Anne-Marie started coughing shortly after. I managed to track down the nurse again and told her about it. Reluctantly, she arranged for suction.

That first evening I did not want to leave until after she had had suction. It was the only way to be sure. Another cause for concern was her feeds. It became obvious that there was no equivalent to the pre-digested milk formula Anne-Marie had been given in Belfast. Here, she was put on Humana 1, a generally available formula-feed. This caused her to have loose bowels.

On this first evening I left about half an hour after the official visiting time had ended. The lights had been turned off and apart from individual spotlights for each bed the ward was dark. I looked back from the door of the side ward and saw a peaceful scene. Anne-Marie's spotlight highlighted St. John the Baptist's icon. The room was transformed by his reassuring presence, his unshakeable assurance of being there, come what may, and by his peace. Even though I would have liked to stay by Anne-Marie's side, I was also able to go in peace, carrying with me the image I had seen when looking back from the door. I knew I was not allowed back in until the next morning.

My old school-friend Andrea, who lives in Munich, came to support me. She came by tube straight from work. It was Tuesday evening, 25 November 1997. Munich was preparing for Christmas. The shops were still open when Andrea and I made our way through the tube system to the city centre. I wanted to buy a pocket-sized German bible, a battery-run cassette recorder, a blank tape and batteries.

A mother who had left a recorder with a children's tape for her daughter, to settle her during the night, had given me an idea. Anne-Marie had been used to being hummed to every time she had been disturbed. I thought to hear mummy's voice somewhere nearby would probably be comforting to her and decided to sing the hymns, choruses and melodies she was used to on tape for her.

We bought the necessary items and then Andrea took me for a beautiful Indian meal. Oh, it was good to be in her company, and to eat lots of mildly spicy food that could *not* be said to taste like cardboard. To my own surprise I enjoyed the meal and was not fretting during the time spent with Andrea. I knew I had left Anne-Marie with St. John the Baptist.

Andrea had come with a folder full of papers for me. There was a map of Munich, a "U Bahn" (tube) map, a new multi-use U Bahn ticket and, very importantly, the residence papers. Anne-Marie and I were now registered as living at her address.

Bully her! She had done lots of running around for us. My thoughtful friend had even made enquiries at the AOK München, the local public health insurance, and had found out which lady would be dealing with us, but our position was anything but clear. Somehow, though, I did not have the same sense of payment panic that so many – especially family members – had. I did not even feel like looking at any of the forms.

I was just glad to have arrived safely, glad to meet Andrea, glad to have got my bible, cassette player, batteries and blank cassette, and thankful too, to have eaten well for the first time in a long while.

Having bid farewell to Andrea I resolved to head back to the McDonald Parents' House to sing and/or hum the little praise songs onto the cassette and then to leave them round to the ward. To get to the McDonald House from the tube station I had to walk past the hospital. I walked up towards the Heart Centre on this cold and dark November night. There was hardly a soul out on the streets. Time had moved on.

I was again grappling with the grandeur of the building and with my feeling hopelessly insignificant in relation to it. I thought of Anne-Marie up there on Level 3 somewhere. My eyes scanned the rooms up on the children's ICU wing. One was lit. I wondered if it might be Anne-Marie's. I stopped walking and wondered where she might be. I looked at the light and imagined that she might sense me getting nearer, that she might be waiting and hoping for me to come and that she needed me.

The dark building did not look welcoming. What would I say to the night porter if he asked me where I was going? I gazed at the modern architecture. There were vertical tubes holding up metal meshwork which was horizontally skirting the different floors. I imagined myself climbing up the outside of the building to get a look at my Anne-Marie. I did not want to have to have discussions with nurses or doctors; I was not looking to upset any rule-stricken Germans. All I wanted was to be peacefully by the side of my baby.

I decided to go on to McDonald House to make the tape to give to her. By this stage I was regretting the time spent over the meal which now seemed so selfish. I could have used it to make the tape and thus have got it to her sooner. All things being equal, I should have been on my way to McDonald House by now. But things were not equal. They were not equal at all. I had become rooted.

I was still at the same spot where my feet had stopped walking, and even though I had firmly decided to go on my feet were not moving. This was a striking new experience for me. My feet and legs, although physically able, would not obey my decision. I was stuck where I was. I had no choice but to stay there and be gentle with myself.

My rational mind wanted to avoid confrontation with the powers that be and to head "home" to make the tape but there was a strong force within me not responding to my decision. I remember even looking down at my feet pondering what they might have in mind to do. I got the impression that they would go towards the hospital if I let them but I was uncomfortable with that idea. I stood on the same spot on this dark and cold November night for quite some time unable to move. Eventually I gave in to the feet and legs, and allowed them slowly, slowly to take me over to the unlit hospital entry.

The revolving door was locked shut but the side door pushed open. I went in and headed over to the lifts. Everything was dark and quiet. Someone called to me enquiring where I was going. It was the night porter. I told him the name of the ward and he did not challenge me any further.

I had to overcome the intercom barrier. What was I to tell them? I told them my name and that I wanted to see Anne-Marie. No one pressed the button. Instead, a nurse came to see me at the door trying to dissuade me from my intention, explaining the visiting times and the hospital policies, saying also that there were too few staff at night to cope with visitors and that I was taking her away from her patients.

I pleaded with her, explaining that I had been allowed to be with Anne-Marie any time I wanted in Belfast and that I had just not got used to their system yet... We had only just arrived and I would only stay a short while and I did not mind if she went to see her patients in the meantime. She said it would have to be clear to me that this was to be strictly an exception and not to be repeated. And so, just in order to get in, I agreed with anything she wanted me to.

Indeed, Anne-Marie had been awaiting me. She was wide-awake and noticed my arriving. I was delighted to see her. This was our first time we met consciously since before setting off from Belfast. I had lots to say to her but I was too aware of being an annoyance to the staff to relax properly.

The nurse gave me space and time alone with Anne-Marie but I felt I should keep to my promise of staying only for a short time in the hope that I would be granted admission again if I behaved reasonably. I left after only five or so minutes, not without explaining my intention of returning later with a cassette player and tape for Anne-Marie.

It had been a long day and I was nearly singing and humming *myself* to sleep as I tried to completely fill both sides of the tape so that nobody would switch it off prematurely. It was after two a.m. when I made my way back to the ward. This time someone pressed the door-open button and I slipped in, gratefully.

I felt encouraged that on this second after-hours night time visit there had not been any real fuss. I was tentatively hopeful that, given time, "they" might just let me see Anne-Marie when I wanted; that they might come round to seeing things my way. I was tired and slept well.

Matthew 14 v.29: "and the disciples picked up twelve basketfuls of broken pieces."

In the morning, there were a number of people sitting at a large table eating their breakfast. I joined them to eat my leftover travel sandwiches. Now in a land of plenty, I immediately stood out as odd for not making a fresh breakfast and maybe also for happily sitting down with them in the expectation of being equal due to our equal or similar circumstances. The reception was aloof, cool and disinterested but through time clusters of people formed and some relationships have endured and look set to continue on into the future.

Philippians 1 v. 29: "For it has been granted to you on behalf of Christ not only to believe on him, but also to suffer for him,"

Visiting times, or rather the restriction of them, turned out to be the greatest cause of suffering for me. How could it be unreasonable for a mother to want to be with her baby, her very seriously ill baby? I had come to some sort of terms with the fact that Anne-Marie was seriously ill but I could not comprehend how I could be wilfully and intentionally stopped from being with her, how I could be regimented into two little slots of visiting times – one a.m. and the other p.m..

Visiting time did not really mean that one was allowed to visit one's child. Often one was allowed to visit the ward, but not the child. During the doctor's ward round parents had to leave and if there had been a new arrival into the same intensive care side ward parents were not allowed in either. That was not entirely new to me.

What *was* new, however, was the regulation that one was not allowed to be anywhere near not only the child but also the side ward when anyone was working with the child. A respectful distance for example during suction was not tolerated. Stepping out of the side ward into the corridor was not tolerated. I was supposed to go down to the end of the corridor and wait to be called. I found this quite unbelievable and while I would have preferred to find it ridiculously laughable, my whole being was incensed and stirred at the injustice of depriving us of each other at our greatest point of need.

This became a deep suffering for me. It was compounded by the fact that nobody could reveal the real reasons for doing things this way. The "explanation" I was invariably given was that this was the way things were done here, that they did not have enough staff to explain everything to inquisitive parents and that other people accepted the rules.

In the five days between our arrival and the operation, there was a steady trickle of minor clashes. I was repeatedly ordered to leave the side ward and to proceed to the end of the corridor. Once or twice I found myself looking in through the window of the corridor. This irritated the nurses.

I had always stayed in order to give moral support to my daughter. But from where I was I could not be heard or seen by Anne-Marie. I had to concede that there was no value in it, except maybe to satisfy my curiosity about what they were doing to Anne-Marie. But curiosity had never before been my motive. I went to where they had sent me. Bit by bit "they" were achieving our forced separation and shaped me to their parent-role image.

Developments, goals, changes in medication, changes in respirator settings, eco-scans, x-rays, bed baths, weighing, suctions, physiotherapies, new lines, blood tests, temperatures, or *anything* else that had happened since the last visit remained secrets guarded by medical and paramedical staff. It felt like betrayal to find out only by lifting off Anne-Marie's blanket that a line had collapsed. And there was nobody to say how the putting-in of the new line had gone, if Anne-Marie had been very distressed or if someone had put her cassette on.

Machines were quietly doing their bit and one was left wondering what was going on at all. When making enquiries, one would hear "she's fine," or "she had a good night." The answer I got was seldom more than one sentence and said in such a way as to minimise the possibility of entering into conversation. From day-to-day it took more of an effort to ask and from day-to-day there was less strength available to be out of unity with the staff. I had been pruned back to manageable size: The quiet mother.

My quest for knowledge about my Anne-Marie's condition had been received with suspicion. Roland told me on the telephone, that one of the doctors had said to him that I did not seem to trust them. The medical information was more easily forthcoming via Roland than through the hospital staff. At least they informed *him*. That had to suffice.

It was 10 p.m. on the day after our arrival before I remembered to look at the daily cleaning-roster-sheet for parents, which hung by the door to the dining room downstairs in McDonald House. I looked at it a couple of times and was not impressed when it said – also the second time – that for Wednesday 26 November 1997 parents in Room No 4 were responsible for cleaning the whole house.

No 4 was my room number. It involved sweeping up in the dining room, mopping up the kitchen and the stairs and hoovering the corridors. I got the hoover out and started to vacuum clean the hall when an irate mother appeared from the common- and dining room, ascertaining that I was mad in the head hoovering at 10 p.m. So I put the hoover away. Suffice to say that I did not brush or mop up either after this experience (a decisive lack of humility here). Instead I cast a generous eye over the surfaces in question and, finding them in no dire need of attention, decided to abandon my attempt at fitting in and giving the expected community service.

As always, Pat was a continuous and invaluable source of love and support over the telephone. He also kept me up to date with our other little darlings, whom I got to speak to on occasions, and with the local news. The children seemed to be coping quite well. Alma had formed a close relationship with Sharon, the neighbour who was looking after her in the mornings. This helped her to cope with missing Mummy.

Having been allowed to see Anne-Marie twice during the first night, I was hopeful that I might be allowed in again during the second night. It turned out to be a reverberating experience....

A while after ringing the buzzer and saying who I was and what I had come for, I was met at the door by – I presume – a doctor. I presumed this as she had a stethoscope around her neck. She greeted me with a wealth of words. She seemed to have a bubbly string of them inside her and they just kept on coming. She was talking excitedly as I was allowed in. She was talking all along the corridor and did not stop talking even when we arrived in Anne-Marie's side ward. She was standing in front of me with her two feet pointing forwards about two to three foot apart, swaying on her straight legs as she delivered her message.

Her message was simple: Everybody abides by the rules. Whether from Denmark or Saudi Arabia, all parents have to stick to visiting times. I put on Anne-Marie's cassette recorder wondering how long it had been lying idle. Her flow of words continued. I assured her that I understood what she was trying to get across but that what *I* was interested in, in order to be able to happily abide by the established rules and regulations, was the *reason* for them being made like this.

I tried my best to say it, without emotional overtones and without sounding accusing. And I *was* genuinely interested, curious and craving to know the reasons for rules that were upheld with such passion. But there were none to be found; there was no pinning her down to answering a straightforward question.

I left after another few minutes of more futile talking, feeling sorry that I had upset another member of staff. I had had no peace to be with Anne-Marie, I had no answers and the whole thing turned out to be farcical. It seemed my genuine motherly motives for seeing Anne-Marie were received as a facetious attempt to cause disruption. I went away saddened. I felt desolate, deprived and dejected, hollow and empty, with nowhere to turn except to God Himself.

Psalm 77 v.2: "When I was in distress I sought the Lord; at night I stretched out untiring hands."

I spent quite some time on my knees in my room that night. I knew that to sing praises would help. So I sang praises to God, kneeling with hands and arms outstretched and raised upward, my head tilted heavenward and my eyes closed. I sang and sang and sang and sang. Bit by bit my disorientated, listless and unsettled state gave way to a more centred, more peaceful and purposeful way of being – God was at work in me while I was singing His praises.

Isaiah 55 v.6: "Seek the Lord while He may be found; Call on Him while He is near"

I turned to my new German Lutheran Bible and opened it aimlessly. There was a new chapter starting in the middle of the page and I began reading from there. It was Chapter 10 of Isaiah. I read the first two verses. In the New International Version (NIV) of the bible they read like this: *"Woe to those who make unjust laws, to those who issue oppressive decrees, to deprive the poor of their rights and withhold justice from the oppressed of my people, making widows their prey, and robbing the fatherless."*

How totally befitting! I was overwhelmed. I was profoundly touched by this reading and totally reassured of God's presence with us. I realised that, although my perception of things seemed to be so painfully un-echoed among some of the parents here, One far more important than any of us was with us and taking our side.

Psalm 119 v. 103, 104:" How sweet are your words to my taste, sweeter than honey to my mouth! I gain understanding from your precepts; therefore I hate every wrong path."

Humbling and reassuring, encouraging and awe-inspiring is the contact with God. I was moved with compassion for the lawmakers. After all, they had probably meant no harm. I felt uneasy at the thought of "woe to them" and decided I would make it my business to do what I could to bring about a change in those laws. It was clear to me that Anne-Marie and I (the widow and the fatherless, with Pat in Belfast) were not to benefit from such efforts, but the thought of sparing other parents and sick children the pain of unnecessary forced separation, coupled with the hope of averting the "woe" from the lawmakers, compelled me to promise my Lord Jesus Christ that I would write a letter to the

Professor in charge, putting forward the case for unrestricted parental visiting times.

I promised this before Anne-Marie's operation but decisively intended to do it no matter how the operation would go, thinking to myself that even if this was the only reason we had come, if something was going to be changed for the better for all concerned, it had been worth coming. I was glad I had made buying a bible my first priority. Reassured of God's presence with us, I slept well.

By the third day all provisions had been used up and it was a case of hurrying to the shops after the a.m. visiting time and then cooking and eating in time for the afternoon slot. I cooked enough to last me for a number of meals, treating eating more like a thing that had to be done than as something to enjoy. With Anne-Marie so seriously ill I could not bear any type of excess. The local 'normal' high standard of living seemed totally inappropriate to me.

I felt so completely at odds with my surroundings that I kept my interaction with them to the absolute minimum: I had not tried to see if the heating in my room was on or not. It would not have entered my head to change the setting. I only put the duvet cover and pillow covers on out of courtesy to the staff of the McDonald House – it would not have mattered to me to sleep without sheets or duvet-cover or pillow-cases.

I missed the hollow worn-out mattress of the Belfast parent room settee where I had had the opportunity to be right there at any time during the day or night. I missed the understanding staff and marvelled at the thought that I might be the only one at odds with the way things were done here.

It got worse. I became reluctant to wash. I felt somehow reassured to smell something of myself in the middle of all that was going on around me, alien as it was. It was winter, and one did not really have occasion to get sweaty, so nobody would have noticed, but I resolved to keep a close eye on myself to see if I was getting depressed or otherwise mentally unstable. This was the first time I experienced this kind of thing and it reminded me of my work experience with mentally ill people, in particular with depressed people some of whom had lost the grip on their personal hygiene altogether. I wondered whether there was some similar mechanism at the bottom of their behaviour.

John 19 v.25: "Near the cross of Jesus stood his mother"

I do not remember any details of the visiting times on the third day but I do remember in some detail how the night time went. It was an outstanding experience that could not have happened had I not had the peace-giving, encouraging and strengthening knowledge of God being right there with us.

The bible reading from Isaiah had found a resounding home in my heart. I had decided to be a tool in His hands for changing the status quo for everybody. Apart from those "higher goals," the mother in me wanted, as always, to be with my daughter. So, on the third night, I set out to sit outside the visitors' entry door of the children's ICU. I did not want to ring the buzzer and I did not want to get into any fruitless arguments with anyone. In fact, I did not feel strong enough to argue with anyone. My aim was not to upset people, but to bear witness to the fact that it is cruel to keep a mother and her sick child apart for no obvious reason. After all, even the mother of Jesus had been allowed to stand near the cross when her son was suffering.

In the absence of chairs I sat down on the marble floor on my old raincoat, in the corner beside the ICU door, reading by the dim light that shone through the big automatic glass door which separated the ICU-tract from the rest of the third floor.

Inwardly chanting the psalms and prayers of the Orthodox prayer book I had brought along with me, I kept a sort of vigil from 10 p.m. to about 2 a.m.. There were not a lot of comings and goings, although a small number of staff passed, entering and leaving the ward through their own door which had an automated combination lock. Some passed saying nothing, others said "hello" or responded to my greeting with a nod of the head.

Suddenly and totally unexpectedly the door beside me opened from the inside and a nurse appeared. For a very short instant I thought she might have come to ask me in but it was very quickly clearly evident that she had no such thing in mind. On the contrary, she had quite definitely come to attack.

Having sat quietly and relatively peacefully for quite a while I was not sufficiently "switched on" to take in all that she was saying. The manner in which she delivered her message struck me more than the actual words she said. It seemed like an onslaught on my quiet corner. My sitting there had obviously irritated her intensely. I got up out of courtesy and tried as best I could to respond in a friendly and non-aggressive way, pointing out quietly that I had not rung the bell, or tried to molest anyone. She had more to say and I listened to her, feeling sorry for her. When she had said all she wanted to say she disappeared again and the door was shut.

The hall returned back to being a solitary, dimly lit quiet place. I sat down again and resumed my previous activity: Reading the psalms, praying and giving praise to God. I had to hold on to the cross to persevere and to be free to do what I saw as God's will for me. The prayers were my tightrope across an abyss of despair and despondency. I could not even raise my eyes to see what might be at the other side: Easter-life, Resurrection-life, the mental image of parents freely coming to visit their little ones at any time of the day or night. It was too distant a goal to carry me by itself. I had to hold on to prayer and especially praise to endure the 'now' and to persevere.

The lady doctor from the previous night came hastily towards the ward and disappeared. There were long stretches of solitude and as it got later and later and I got more and more tired, I started to doubt the value of my vigil. I coaxed myself into holding out longer by setting goals in my prayer book, i.e., just another two pages, and when they were done, just another two pages …

This is what I was doing when two doctors came out of the ward, and heading out had to pass me, facing me. I had briefly met one of them before. I gathered he would have been something akin to a Senior House Officer. He was a very tall, youngish man with peculiarly shaped glasses. He came over to talk to me. He came over oozing concern and compassion for this little huddled up heap of a mother that was me. His genuine warmth came so unexpectedly that it took me completely unawares. I had been prepared for anything except for a sympathetic heart, full of love. The recognition of his kindly outlook instantly choked me.

Tears were welling up within me that I could not control. I had lost my voice and literally could not physically answer his questions except by nodding my head or by shaking it. Tears started running down my face and I felt like a little schoolgirl. I had not got up from where I was sitting and he had not got down to my level, yet his genuine concern bridged the huge physical distance.

Seeing that I could not give him any answers or have a conversation with him, he decided to continue on his way with his colleague who had watched at a little distance. I remained sitting there but with my eyes filled with tears I could not see the writing in my prayer book.

Another unmeasured time passed and the door beside me was opened again. A nurse was standing in the door asking me what I wanted. This time I did not jump to my feet. I remained sitting down, just shook my head, and said as best I could without choking: "You know what I want." She talked about visiting times and disappeared again. I stayed for another little while and then decided to return to the McDonald House to go to sleep. My mission for that day had been done.

I went to bed tired and feeling a little lonely. I was wondering about the value of what I had done and was open to some encouragement and reassurance. Immersed in these thoughts and feelings I spotted a little ladybird walking along my bed. In the middle of winter! It was a delight. It spoke to me of the love of the Father. I had not been forgotten or abandoned. I let the little fellow walk on to my hand. Thankfulness and peace, even joy filled my soul. I set him down on a huge spreading plant out in the corridor just opposite my room and hoped he (she?) might find something to keep himself alive there. I slept well.

My night escapade did not go unnoticed. The next day the kind Swiss ward sister wanted to talk to me. I conveyed to her that I found it hard to imagine that I would be the only parent in favour of unrestricted visiting times. She offered me a consultation with the hospital's psychologist which, even in the knowledge that this might put me into a neat little box (i.e. deranged), I welcomed decidedly cheerfully, and thanked her for the suggestion. An appointment outside the ward visiting hours was arranged.

It was a relief to see the psychologist. She was very much in support of a change of visiting times and encouraged me to write my letter to the clinic director. She had been trying to change the approach here for quite some time, but so far her ideas had fallen on deaf ears. She quoted a German saying: "Der stete Tropfen höhlt den Stein,"– "the steady drip hollows the stone." The hope was that with repeated requests for unrestricted visiting resistance to it would wear progressively thinner, and eventually a change would come.

I told her of the Bible reading and she was open to acknowledging that God was very close. I also mentioned how precious the time spent with Anne-Marie was to me, and how, with the normal workings of the ward, one had no guarantee of seeing one's child even during the short visiting times. With Anne-Marie's life in the balance in the forthcoming operation, I craved to savour every moment with her. Every minute in her company was a cause to quietly celebrate our time and our life together. Being robbed of the chance of living like this gave me pain and grief.

The psychologist was very supportive and understanding and said she would speak to the senior clinic director, Professor Hess, to see if he might allow me to spend more time with Anne-Marie, especially in view of her uncertain future. That all sounded very good. There was an atmosphere of mutual respect and support which I had missed up until then. It was a relief to meet someone who cared in a way that I could understand and relate to.

The response from the clinic leadership, delivered the following day, was that Anne-Marie was not in immediate danger of losing her life and that there was no case for introducing special regulations for us.

It made me a little sad when later, on the evening before her operation, I was given permission (without having asked for it) to stay longer than usual with Anne-Marie. Did "they" really think that the time leading up to this had not been equally important? Should not every moment spent with another human being be intensely valuable – a sanctifying moment in which the Christ in me meets with the Christ in you? Is consistency of love less valuable than last minute top-ups? Needless to say, my desire to be with her easily overruled any half- thoughts of not availing of the given opportunity. But it felt artificial to be offered it, just then.

Of course, life has more value in the face of death, and there is a greater urgency to live according to our inmost convictions in the face of death. But are we not all constantly living in the face of death - but for the Grace of God, who gives us life? Surely it must be one of our aims to become and remain aware of this in order to live every moment without losing any opportunity to love.

One lunchtime prior to the operation an echo-scan teaching demonstration used Anne-Marie as the patient. The teacher and his pupils waltzed in, and for whatever reason, neglected to send me out. Perhaps they were so involved in their work, that they had simply not noticed me. While scanning Anne-Marie's heart they were explaining things about "his" heart. I suppose there is a 50/50 chance to get it right if everyone is talked about as being male.

There was no "hello" to Anne-Marie or to me, nor any other sign of recognition of the fact that the heart they were looking at belonged to a living human being. It made me wonder about the true motives for medical advance. Is it really to help *people* or is it fuelled rather by some sort of fascination of what can be done with the use of expertise and machines and then justified in the public eye thanks to the lucky by-product that it could also help people?

Slowly the parents in McDonald House were becoming a more mutually supportive group and I spent a few evenings in the common-room with other parents. The abiding memory of this is the clarity with which the downsides of television-viewing imprinted themselves on my mind.

A most worrying aspect about viewing at this prime time of the evening for me was the fact that it was easy to get sucked into viewing whatever was on, *in the hope that something better might come on*! I spent a number of evenings like this throughout our stay in Munich. Programmes seemed to come up with more and more weird ideas to keep the attention of the viewers (such as a man dressed as a frog jumping across the desks of clerical workers in an open-plan office). Of course, violence and other deranged aspects of humanity featured greatly in the later hours, but I was unable to stay and watch those sorts of things.

The most insidious aspect of watching TV was the fact that when I finally did go up to my room, it was eleven o'clock instead of nine and my head was filled with rubbish. It took longer to come to a prayerful attitude and, being that bit later, the temptation to give in to tiredness and to economise on contact with the eternal source of love, truth and strength was certainly there. This would have made Anne-Marie and me and our situation as well as any other persons or situations benefiting from my prayers the victims of my evening's TV viewing.

With the operation looming ahead of us, my mother, understandably not wanting to let Roland end up with a huge bill, contacted the German tabloid press. Upon hearing about a "hardship fund" set up by one of the most repulsive of them she had talked over the phone to a lady connected with it and had received a favourable response. So long as they were going to get the story they would consider giving money.

Aware that I was not over-anxious to write the story for them, my mother had written an account herself, typed it and sent it to me to sign. I felt sickened at the thought of taking money from the paper in question and stored her papers in my bedside cabinet with the rest of the forms, until I should have more clarity about what to do. My half-secret hope was that the E-form we had requested in Belfast might yet be granted and might - miraculously, so to speak - solve everything.

1 December 1997, the date of the proposed operation, was advancing. I wanted to make contact with the local Christian ministers to get a blessing for Anne-Marie through them. As she had mainly had contact with Catholic clergy at home I thought I would now make contact with the Protestant and Orthodox leaves of the shamrock (or clover).

The Protestant Minister was the mother of a number of children. She came to visit and pray and was supportive in a bubbly sort of way. Having had the experience of a highly dangerous operation with one of her own children, she had first-hand knowledge about standing up for parental rights. She prayed for a blessing for Anne-Marie, and gave us a candle for the big day.

I also made my way to the Russian Orthodox Monastery of St. Job of Pocaev by public transport one evening but the lengthy trip yielded no tangible results for Anne-Marie. They did not seem anxious to come to a hospital at the other end of the city to give a blessing to someone who was not even Orthodox.

Back in my parent room I opened my bible at the prophet Daniel and read: (Chapter 10 v. 19), *"Do not be afraid, O man highly esteemed,"* he said, *"Peace! Be strong now; be strong." When he spoke to me I was strengthened…"* As I read these words I was indeed strengthened and exceedingly humbled before God.

The Operation

Dr Peters, the paediatric cardiologist who had met us at the airport, took me into his office to sign the consent form for the planned operation. Seated behind a huge table he outlined a number of possible problems. Anne-Marie could be left dependant on a pacemaker, as due to the close proximity of the conducting nodes to the site of the proposed operation, these nodes, which regulate the heartbeat, could get damaged. There were other dangers, too, and of course nobody could guarantee that she would come through the operation alive. He was careful to imprint this on my mind.

Upon enquiring about any procedures that would be necessary in case of her death I learned that I may then be asked permission to allow some tissues to be removed for research and that I would be assisted in making funeral arrangements. Pat and I had agreed that if she were to die in Germany, Anne-Marie would be buried with her cousin Nora, my sister's third child, who had died during birth and had been laid to rest in Bonn.

I signed on the dotted line and enquired if Anne-Marie's icon of St. John the Baptist could accompany her into the operating theatre. Dr Peters thought this should be possible, but suggested I should ask the surgeon, Professor Meisner, who was to come to speak to me later.

Professor Meisner found me at Anne-Marie's bedside. He respectfully allowed her icon to be present in the theatre during the operation. He also made sure that I understood that there were no guarantees. He looked deeply into my eyes and soul, and saw that I understood. I was not receptive to hearing details about the operation and accordingly it was a brief encounter.

My sister Verena arrived on Sunday 30 November '97, the day before the operation. She came with her own poster copy of St. John the Baptist's icon and her guitar, to accompany our songs of praise and worship. By special permission, so to speak in place of Pat, she was allowed to visit Anne-Marie. She was disturbed to see Anne-Marie the way she was - a helpless, exposed and suffering little bundle, at the mercy of God, who was presently working through hi-tech modern medicine for her.

It had been a sudden change for Verena. Coming from her bustling four-children-household the quietness here greatly affected her. I was at home with silence by now and reluctant to become uncentred through Verena's many questions and well-meaning suggestions.

My family wanted to settle the financial side of things as quickly as possible. They did not want to wait for a form that might never come. Their anxiety threatened to unsettle me. To appease Verena, on the day of her arrival we went to the hospital administration and to the Social Services and explored possibilities for raising the necessary funds. The outlook was bleak. Yet I had to put all these things to the back of my mind to allow me to live intensively in tune with Anne-Marie.

The evening before Anne-Marie's operation I *was* grateful for the extra time with her. Nobody knew what tomorrow would bring. It was difficult to choose the right time to go, having been deprived of this freedom up to then. I returned to McDonald House a little later than usual. The next morning I was allowed in early to spend another little while with my darling and to accompany her to the operating theatre. The operation was expected to last most of the day and I was to give the ICU a ring at 12 noon for the first progress report.

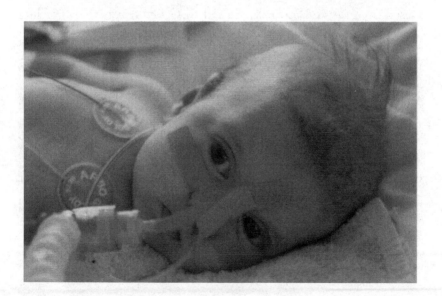

Anne-Marie was fully alert, her eyes fixed on mine as her cot was pushed down the corridors, never once letting go as we entered and travelled in the lift. Her eyes clung onto mine all the way to the operating theatre, and mine, too, were absorbed with looking at hers, never once looking to the right or the left, not even when the nurse was speaking to me.

I wanted to stay with Anne-Marie until she lost consciousness, not to abandon her, but I was not allowed to accompany her into the operating theatre. She was pushed in, her eyes clinging onto mine until the doors closed behind her. A look that to this day has engraved itself on my heart.

The icon of St. John had gone with her, and now there was nothing more I could do, except to turn to God. I went down to the hospital chapel to pray and knelt down in front of the altar. I closed my eyes and inwardly turned to God. It was there, feeling "I-don't-know-how", that a ray of light from above shone into me. I heard God asking: "... *well?*" I took this to be His invitation to ask Him for what I had not outrightly asked for since she had got so very ill. I said "Let her live, Lord, let her live, please."

That was it. I had felt invited to make my petition and I had made it. I did not stay much longer but got up and went over to McDonald House to return to my sister. We intended to spend the day singing God's praises together.

I was greeted by a pile of broken glass on the floor of my room. A picture had come off the wall. Why would Verena touch pictures in a room that was not hers and not even really mine either? I was irritated and insisted that she should have to replace the broken glass. My annoyance did not subside until she said, "I think it fell off and shattered at the time of the first incision." She had sensed this as the glass shattered. Reconstructing the events we found that it could well have coincided time-wise.

I apologised. As soon as I was able to see the hand of God in the events, my hardness melted. My sister, like any of us, was subject to the will of God happening through her. Apparently she had tried to hang up *her* copy of St. John's icon by sticking its two backward-folded upper corners behind the picture frame when the picture fell off the wall.

We made our way over to the hospital chapel, guitar and icon in hand. I also brought a songbook with Charismatic Renewal songs (for the most part based on psalms or other bible passages) and we also used the German praise book which was in the chapel. Verena joined easily into the English songs and we sang more and more freely. We sang in harmony, in unity. We sang wholeheartedly, without holding back, letting go of all inhibitions, I gave it my all. This was not a concert or a show - this was complete surrender to God, to the fervent praise of Him, having pulled up all the stops.

One of the songs we sang is based on psalm 134 (Western numbering):

1.Praise the Lord

all you servants of the Lord
you who minister by night within his courts
lift up your hands within the sanctuary
and praise theLord.

2. May this Lord, the maker of heaven and earth,
may this Lord, bless you from Zion
lift up your hands within the sanctuary
and praise the Lord (we Praise You Lord)
(Alleluia, we praise You Lord).

In the middle of this song, quite without any prior notice, my spirit rose within me toward God and in an instant, just when powerfully and involuntarily streaming upward from my heart along my throat and mouth, it was united with a touch of the Power of God, reaching downward and inward, along the same path, to the very core of my being. I felt Verena looking over. She sensed that something was happening.

In the form of a flash-like memory I was reminded of a similar incident when singing in a folk-choir in our local Catholic Church in Belfast. One day I had been unable to get into the right spirit for singing praise and was a little despondent at my lack of "Spirit and Truth" when something like a ray of God's light fell on me, giving me the right Spirit instantly. Again, at that very same time, a spiritually sensitive person, sitting about three people away from me, stretched their neck to look over to me to see what was happening.

Adjoining the chapel wall was Sr. Miriam's office. This joyful, light, slight, and gentle nun, who was the Catholic Hospital

Chaplain, must have been disturbed in her work by our singing. She came to join us and asked about Anne-Marie.

At a later stage I was glad to be able to give my 'tithe' to her. I had separated the tenth part of all moneys I had been given. Encouraged and amazed about my dedication to this practice, even in the face of not knowing how the hospital bills would get paid, she passed the money on to where it was needed. I felt very strongly that if I continued to be faithful to this practice God would see to the rest.

Sr. Miriam sang with us and we lost track of time. It was after 12 noon when she reminded us to make enquiries about Anne-Marie. We bade our farewells and headed up to the Intensive Care Ward where we were met by Dr Peters. He said: "Yes, she's already back on the ward, everything has gone well, you can go and see her if you wish."

Of course I wanted to see her! But first things first. The ten cured lepers, of whom only one returned to give thanks to God, came to my mind. We took the lift down again and knocked on Sr. Miriam's door. Flying into her arms, full of joy, we asked her to join us in a thanksgiving song. She, too, was delighted and we learnt and sang together one of her favourite songs, called "Christus Sieger" which means: "Christ (is the) victor"- a most beautiful proclamation of His Lordship.

Glory and praise to God. The operation was over and all had gone far better than anyone dared to hope. It had been completed successfully in *less than half the expected time*. There was a big hill before us yet, of course: The recovery, but for now all had gone well, very well. Thank you, God.

The sun was streaming into the ICU side ward and lit up the little intensive care "bed" where Anne-Marie was lying. It was a peaceful and joyful scene, the snow outside adding extra brightness to the light.

Anne-Marie lay peacefully sleeping under the influence of the anaesthetic, connected to the respirator. There was a thick, transparent plastic tube coming out from underneath her sternum, from underneath the white dressing over her wound. One could watch the blood rise and fall in it with every heartbeat. Various signs and bits of information were written on the white dressing and a pacemaker was still connected in case it would be needed.

We spent a while watching the blood rising and falling in the plastic tube, soaking up the miracle, quiet in the presence of the outcome which spelt out life, a new gift or lease of life.

I was told that she had been fitted with quite a good size of valve considering her tender age and correspondingly tiny heart and that they had been able to close the various holes between her heart chambers. Everybody was very pleased with how the operation had gone. Also, the valve was a pig's valve which meant that there would be no need to take any daily anti-coagulants such as Warfarin or Aspirin.

Back to restricted visiting times, and to trying to sort out the financial side of things, Verena got a written estimate of the cost of this life-saving operation and hospital stay from the Clinic Director, Professor Hess. She also bought a frame with a glass pane and left me a lovely postcard of a red chalk drawing of "Anna" by Leonardo da Vinci. This was a portrait showing a beautiful gentle smile. It was "Anna" the mother of Mary, and the grandmother of Jesus.

Doctors and nurses remarked that Anne-Marie's recovery was textbook-style, without hitches of any sort. She reached the point where she was expected to be able to go without the respirator more quickly than some children with lesser operations. My little bundle! The removal of the respirator brought back memories of how difficult and stressful it had been for her to breathe without it in the ICU in Belfast.

A veteran nurse was attending Anne-Marie that day in Munich. She was a rough diamond but experienced and knew what she was doing. She breezed in and out regularly during the most critical time, keeping an eye not only on the monitor and the blood-gas results but also on Anne-Marie herself. According to the monitor screen, blood-gasses were beginning to fall outside the normally acceptable range, yet our nurse spoke from experience when she muttered: "Different ones can cope with different levels," implying that Anne-Marie was as yet coping.

Anne Marie was working hard to breathe. Breathing was Anne-Marie's full-time task and she lay there doing just that. Our nurse's knowledge and feel for the situation were eventually rewarded by the blood gas-levels returning to within the acceptable range and continuing to hold throughout the night. Anne-Marie did not need to be intubated again.

Oma and Opa (German for Granny and Granddad) came to Munich on the 5 December, five days after the operation. Amazingly, they had organised this five-hour journey even before Anne-Marie was born. Oma was allowed to see her granddaughter by special permission.

Anne-Marie looked pitiful - small and so still - except for her laboured breathing. I formally introduced them to each other, and Anne-Marie took careful note of Oma, looking straight into her eyes, and taking in the essence of the person that was her grandmother. A look which simultaneously radiated wisdom, peace and knowledge, all in the midst of suffering, illness and near exhaustion. My mother often tried to describe this encounter. It made a lasting impression on her.

Anne-Marie's recovery was progressing well and Dr Lorenz considered moving Anne-Marie out of intensive care, pointing out how costly each ICU day was. He was concerned for Roland, who was the guarantor for payment. I saw a new, more personal side to this professional man. I got a glimpse into a kind heart.

After all, without his personal dedication, Anne-Marie would not have been allowed to come. It was *he* who had decided to take her, in the good faith that somehow the bill would get paid. Not everybody would have had the courage and compassion to do this! I began to realise that my initial experience when coming to Munich had made me less able to see and appreciate this man's efforts to be helpful within this, very different, framework. I felt sorry that I had – to whatever degree – caused disruption also for this fine, caring man.

At long last a letter from Belfast arrived, *with the appropriate E-form in it!* I phoned Roland who then contacted the local AOK (German general health insurance). He briefed me about his phone call and the next morning I submerged myself into the early morning rush-hour stream of the underground system. I arrived at the AOK before they opened to the public and spent my waiting time enclosed in a phone box.

Sheltered from the cold and singing praises to God I watched the morning rise. Fine tufts of white clouds were gracing the fresh light blue of the early morning sky. Every once-in-a-while I practised the Greek-sounding name of the lady who was to attend to us. Thanks to Roland, when the doors finally opened, I was able to join the stream of people who all knew where to go. Butterflies outside the door; …a final practice of her name before knocking and going in.

It was a spacious bright open-plan office with a number of clerical workers. One or two looked up to see who had come in. All the practice had paid off. The Greek name rolled off my tongue with ease and a friendly-looking young woman got up immediately and came over to attend to me. She knew about my coming through Roland's phone call.

I gave her my E-form and asked her for AOK cover for myself and for Anne-Marie, which she was happy to give. Something had to be signed, here and there; some instructions were given, these forms were to be taken to the GP, and those were to be used in case of hospital treatment, the hospital would then fill in this part. She was making sure I knew what to do with all of them. She was so kind! I felt like hugging her and dancing round the office with her for joy and happiness but of course I just sat there trying to listen to her instructions which ended with, "if you have any difficulties you can always come back." She certainly had a heart for new arrivals in Germany.

I floated out of the office. This was it! The cost of the operation, of the hospital stay, of all the treatment would be covered! I had the forms in my hand. Nobody would have to sell any cars or pianos and we would not have to use any money from the tabloid press or other untoward sources. Glory to God! The ladies in the hospital administration were delighted for us, too, and started to process the forms immediately.

Anne-Marie's incredible operation and recovery-experience had made waves, and had raised the general interest level in us. Towards the end of the ICU time communication was much improved. This was also due to meetings with the ward sister and with the psychologist who in turn were liaising with the doctors.

After Anne-Marie's transferral to the 'normal' young children's heart ward Verena's beautiful postcard of Anna watched over Anne-Marie's head end, while St. John the Baptist was minding the foot end. Anna looked lovingly and caringly down at my little bundle in the cot and became a talking point especially with a nurse of the same name, who was touched by the gentle image.

Here, too, all visitors had to wear special gowns, and children were not allowed to visit. Parents of more than one child had a difficult time. With Daddy at work, when Mummy came to visit her sickly one on the ward, she could leave the little brother or sister in the unattended playroom outside the automatically locked ward doors…(?)

Anne-Marie and I had a few visitors from around Munich and from further afield. It was good to be able to take them to see Anne-Marie. Pia, our Swiss bridesmaid and godmother of Pascal came by train from Zurich. When she had tiny Anne-Marie on her arm, they were smiling right into each other's eyes. It was wonderful to witness. Despite his busy eye surgery schedule Roland, too, came to visit. After all he had done for us he was finally meeting up with Anne-Marie!

Psalm 139 v. 16: "All the days ordained for me were written in your book before one of them came to be.

Anne-Marie was getting stronger and livelier and I was allowed to bath and dress her. I had disconnected her from the monitor and was standing by the changing area with her when an old school friend, now living in Munich, arrived. My friend sat down by Anne-Marie's cot. In an instant, I had a powerful deja-vu experience. I felt very intensely that I had lived through exactly the same situation before. Searching my memory I was nearly sure that I had dreamt it years ago.

All sorts of thoughts and questions arose in my mind. What is reality? What is time? Are our lives mapped out to the last detail before we live them? How self-determined is our "free will"? For some reason it seemed obvious to me then, that "time" did not actually exist, but that it was a non-entity made up for the benefit of giving us humans orientation and a framework, as we are so limited that we can only live one thing "at a *time*." I found this mind-boggling and exhilarating.

Anne-Marie's progress continued to be steady, even though she did not manage to suck more than 20 ml of milk per feed for quite some time. Even after discharge she was still dependent on her naso-gastric tube for the greater parts of her feeds. This tube was a real blessing now and I could indeed feed Anne-Marie through it mostly without disturbing her, even when she was sleeping.

To tube-feed her, a funnel was attached to the end of the tube and filled with warmed-up formula milk. Carefully holding it at the right height ensured a constant, slow dribble of milk into her stomach. The medicines, too, were given via the tube and then flushed down using sterile water to make sure they were not just medicating the tube.

Now that the breathing tube was no longer occupying Anne-Marie's throat, she started to make occasional tentative noises. These got more purposeful as time went on but were never strong enough to make herself heard outside the confines of the side ward. It took her much longer to realize that she could now also move her head. Back at home, the first time she freely turned her head when lying on her back turned out to be a major revelation to her!

With Anne-Marie continuing to make an excellent recovery, the emergency feel of our situation was lifting and my body seized the opportunity to ask for attention: Quite out of the blue and without obvious reason I felt very sick. I had not eaten anything bad or heard of any bugs going around. I vomited in the hospital toilets and many more times into different bushes as I staggered along my short way back to the parent accommodation.

Any casual by-passer would have had to be forgiven for concluding that I must have been on the drink. (How easy it is to draw wrong conclusions.)

Arriving at McDonald House I realised that this was my day for cleaning the house again. Thankfully the caretaker agreed to do it instead. Thank God. I went to bed pondering my sickness. From the day of Anne-Marie's birth until now, I had been in very unusual and demanding circumstances. I felt this was my body saying: "Now that the worst part is over, allow me to let you know how I feel about all of this." I needed to grant it rest and to be gentle with myself. I just slept. The next day I was much better, even though still queasy.

Things had to be done. In the absence of computers, flight enquiries had to be made over the telephone. There had been talk of getting home for Christmas. I felt sure that at such short notice the flights for the Christmas holidays would all be booked up. I was to check out scheduled flights from Munich to London-Heathrow, and from there back to Belfast.

There was also the dilemma of discharge versus transfer. If Anne-Marie were to be *transferred* to the Royal Sick Children's Hospital she would need to be accompanied by a doctor. If she were to be *discharged* we would travel alone. There was no question about going straight home. Everybody agreed that Anne-Marie should be seen in the hospital upon return to give Belfast doctors the chance of acquainting themselves with her again, with her feeding situation, the new valve and medication, etc.

It was not usual practice to discharge while expecting admission elsewhere, but after some "hmms" and "haas," an exception to the rule was made on the condition that an ambulance would meet us at Belfast Airport and speed us to Clark Clinic. I was to book our tickets nearer the time, to be sure Anne-Marie would be well enough to travel.

John 8 v.47: "He who belongs to God hears what God says."

One day I was just leaving a bag of groceries in my parent-room when my telephone rang. This was unusual. Usually it rang in the evenings when someone was kindly returning my call to lessen my expenditure. As it was, the phone was ringing in the middle of the day. I went over to pick it up. A person at the other end explained who she was – she was a theatre nurse who had assisted during the operation.

She had rung my number repeatedly but there had never been any reply. She thought she would ring again, just one more time to try to reach me before she was heading home to Ireland for Christmas the following day. For some reason I felt overjoyed that she phoned me, and I just told her of Anne-Marie's special story, whether she wanted to know it or not. It was just bubbling out of me.

Stirred by what she heard, she acknowledged that this story confirmed her in her reason for ringing. She had suspected that there might have been more to it! She had phoned again and again to let me know what Professor Meisner had said in the operating theatre, after finishing the operation. She explained (in English) that he had remarked about *"a very special presence during the operation"* and that he had stated: *"Anne-Marie is definitely a holy child."*

What a phone-call! What a faithful nurse had assisted this special operation! Bless the Lord O my soul! And, touched by the Holy Spirit and without looking to his own honour, Professor Meisner, this humble man, had acknowledged *"a very special presence"* as well as *"a holy child."* This internationally acclaimed Professor of Cardiac Surgery later on would not accept my thanks for the operation but instead repeatedly insisted: *"A miracle has happened,"* even though he played an essential part in this miracle. *Bless the Lord, O my soul!*

You appointed this faithful man who allowed You to carry out Your will through him, and who gave You the Glory. *Praise and bless the Lord, O my soul and forget not all His benefits – Who forgives all your sins and heals all your diseases, Who redeems your life from the pit and crowns you with love and compassion, Who satisfies your desires with good things, so that your youth is renewed like the eagle's. Praise and Bless the Lord, O my soul,* who appointed this faithful woman, untiring in trying to impart to me the words spoken through the Holy Spirit. ...*Bless the Lord, O my soul,* who sent me to the parent-room with my bit of shopping just when she rang one last time before flying home the next day...*Praise the Lord, O my soul – all my inmost being, praise His Holy Name. Praise Him for His faithful people, praise Him for*

His perfect ways, praise Him in the highest heavens. Praise Him on the earth below. Praise the Lord, you His angels You mighty ones who do His bidding, Who obey His word Praise the Lord, all His heavenly hosts, you servants, who do His will. Praise the Lord, all His works everywhere in His dominion. Praise the Lord, O my soul.

My heart overflowed with joy – I was elated. Tears filled my eyes. I wanted to share His blessings, to share this joy, this good news, with someone. My mother was instantly deeply touched and recorded all the things I told her, immediately getting pen and paper to hand, so that nothing would get lost or changed through time. My sister, too, found tears of joy welling up within her and when our old (80+ year old) Russian Orthodox friend Tamara Korkashvili heard about Professor Meisner's description of Anne-Marie as "definitely a holy child," she just said, very lovingly, "Sure, we knew that all along."

Matthew 16 v. 15-17 "Who do you say I am?" Simon Peter answered, "You are the Christ, the Son of the living God." Jesus replied, "Blessed are you, Simon son of Jonah, for this was not revealed to you by man, but by my Father in heaven."

Never before had it been so clear to me that it took a touch of the Holy Spirit to recognise the work of God. Without this touch of the Spirit of God we are blind to sanctity and holiness, around and about us. Yet Jesus also *"warned His disciples not to tell anyone that He was the Christ."*

Similarly, I was only able to disclose Professor Meisner's statement of Anne-Marie being definitely a holy child to a small number of people, mentioning to others only about the "special presence" and about the "miracle" he had referred to. Deeply grateful to Professor Meisner I needed to thank him. Both he and Dr. Lorenz received the best I could give to anybody – CDs of Orthodox choir music.

It was confirmed that I should book a flight before Christmas! Incredible. Some other children who had been operated on before Anne-Marie were still in intensive care and here was Anne-Marie, deemed ready to spend Christmas back in Belfast, less than a month after taking off from there under quite different circumstances. I requested assisted transfer in Heathrow and arranged to be picked up by ambulance in Belfast to go straight to Clark Clinic.

It was 22 December 1997. A McDonald parents' house guest book entry had to be written. St. John the Baptist's icon, the new picture-frame minus the glass and the rest of my belongings, which had notably increased, had to be packed and last but not least, the parent room and bathroom were to be thoroughly cleaned. Somehow things have a habit of building up on the last day. I left the room tidy, the beds stripped, drawers empty but did not get time to do any cleaning. Disclosing this to the housekeeper, who was finishing off my bill for my stay, meant that I did not get my deposit for the room back. Ah well.

Having come without a buggy I had to carry Anne-Marie as well as one bag with the icon, one with my belongings and a little rucksack with essential things for the journey for Anne-Marie. Andrea left us to the airport in good time and the British Airways staff put us on the plane before the rest of the passengers.

One of the stewardesses came to sit with us for a little chat. When she heard about the heart operation and the miraculous outcome she was so truly moved, delighted and overjoyed for us, that she went and got presents for us from BA. She gave Anne-Marie a lovely little cuddly bear, which later became her favourite toy, and handed me a bag full of little bottles of Champagne saying "These are for you and your husband to celebrate when you get home." She told the other members of the crew and we got full VIP treatment from all of them for the duration of that flight.

Anne-Marie was alert and interested in everything with her lovely eyes looking out of her little thin face. She looked so small and so light, so slight and delicate, with her feeding-tube fastened to her nose. - It was quite a change for her from spending her day lying in her hospital cot!

Back to Base

It was 22 December 1997. Anne-Marie's cot was ready in Clark Clinic and Sr. Alison was getting me a mattress for the children's toy room so that I would not need to be too far away. How pleasant to be back where your wishes mattered. I was not used to this kind of thing any more and it touched me. I was in need of lying down. By the time a mattress was found and put down, my head had started to spin – the walls of the ward were wobbling. I was getting vertigo. I told them everything was perfect and just lay down – away into deep sleep.

How wonderful to be wakened by a nurse when Anne-Marie's feeding time came! How lovely to be included, to be allowed to be the real mummy again. Under different circumstances this middle-of-the-night scenario would perhaps seem undesirable but for me at that time this was the real coming home. It was a delight to be holding my little darling on my lap again and to try her with a little more milk. The reality of the mother and child bond was allowed to come to the fore again. Glory to God.

The following day we had our family reunion. What a picture to see my four darlings coming down the corridor of Clark Clinic. Raphael, Pascal, Alma and Papa! Raphael started running when he saw me. I ended up sitting on the toy-room floor with the children climbing all over me and Papa looking on, standing by. He had not expected to see Anne-Marie again. One of the nurses later told a colleagues about the wonderful welcome we had received from the children – her fingers just drew two lines down from her eyes, and she turned away to do something else.

Everybody was so very happy to see little Anne-Marie. It became obvious, that neither staff nor family had really expected to see her again. Yet I was not too keen for our children to get too close as there was a tummy bug in our house. This was the beginning of a seemingly constant battle against bugs and against passing them on. And although at times I took this to somewhat extreme lengths, Anne-Marie spent her first year largely going in and out of hospital with various different kinds of infections.

We were discharged home on 24 December after getting the medication sorted out. Back in our little cramped and overfilled car the windows steamed up - our little family on the way home. Everything, even every-day nuisances, seemed precious. The children were so pleased to have us home again that for the best part of the first day or two they even tried very hard not to fight with each other!

It was Christmas. Santa had unmistakably come. Stored away toys which had arrived in one way or another throughout the year graced the bottom of the Christmas tree. Neighbours, friends and relatives, too, had been very generous. But Anne-Marie remained the star of the feast.

Anne-Marie and I were kept busy with a host of regular small feeds, medication and nappies, etc. We moved into the downstairs front room while Papa and the children lived upstairs. He was doing his nightshifts upstairs, while I was doing mine downstairs. Of course, Alma was still in nappies, too.

Papa had been a wonderful manager of work, house, farm and everything to do with the children. My task now was to make adequate care-time for my two preschool girls at home, looking after our two little schoolboys and generally taking some family responsibilities off Papa's shoulders as he was resuming his full-time work. Thankfully Pat continued to be very flexible and when there was no dinner made when he came home he just made one. Nothing seemed too much trouble for him and still is not.

On one occasion, when we were pondering the gift of Anne-Marie's life together, I remarked to him quite out of the blue and much to my own surprise that she had come through *this* operation all right but that she would die at a later one -- words which I remembered after our return from Birmingham.

At this, her first Christmas, Anne-Marie remained quite well, although she was still sweaty to the touch – a symptom of heart problems in children. However, before too long she had picked up some of the bugs that were circulating in our house and we spent New Year's Eve and the first few days of January 1998 back in hospital.

Proverbs 31 v. 8 & 9: "Speak up for those who cannot speak for themselves, for the rights of all who are destitute. Speak up and judge fairly: defend the rights of the poor and needy."

This hospital stay gave me the time I needed to put pen to paper and to make good the promise I had made to my Lord to write a letter about visiting times to the Munich hospital director Professor Hess. Professor Hess, himself a Dutchman, professed to speak better English than German; so I decided to write my appeal in English.

In the letter I explained that I would not be writing it at all, had I not promised to do so to Our Lord. I then praised the present facilities of the McDonald House, which had surely been provided in recognition of the fact that parents should be near their children, especially when these are ill.

With reference to Mary, mother of Jesus, at the foot of the cross, I explored two approaches to parental visiting times– *one* of removing parents from any "nasty" medical procedures in order not to be associated with them by their children, and *the other* of giving children support by means of the presence of their parents especially during those procedures. I suggested allowing *parents* to choose between these approaches rather than imposing the clinic's view upon them. The letter was ready for posting on the day we were discharged home.

Having benefited from the time away together, Anne-Marie and I returned to our hectic and noisy home. It was always an adjustment for all concerned. The children had to learn very fast to be considerate to the special needs of their little sister. Nitty-gritty day-to-day realities had to be lived without new high points of outstanding miracles.

The children had to learn to be so quiet that they would not waken Anne-Marie when she was sleeping. They learned covering their mouths when coughing, and putting their tissues into the bin after blowing their noses - rather than leaving them lying about as generous sources of free-for-all bugs. Thankfully nobody wanted Mummy and Anne-Marie to be in hospital so they all tried their best to accommodate their pale, thin and weak looking little sister. They enjoyed her company when she was awake and liked to try to engage her in play or to amuse her by little tricks and funny stunts, which she appreciated greatly.

Luke 2 v. 19: "But Mary treasured up all these things and pondered them in her heart."

One later Advent season I realised how Anne-Marie had amplified my understanding of the infant Christ. When someone remarked how the tender infant Jesus must have had no idea of all the things he was to go through in later life, my experience of Anne-Marie, who at the age of seven weeks indicated to go to Munich, compelled me to go beyond my previous concepts. If Anne-Marie knew something of her destiny, surely Jesus would have known all of what lay ahead of him even in infancy. How much more humbling for us that he went on to do what he had come for without allowing himself to get distracted from his harrowing path.

Gradually Anne-Marie's Duocal-enriched-milk intake increased and with longer intervals between the feeds, my night duty was reduced to only one feed. We had to aim for a minimum total per day and kept a careful record of every five millilitres she took, totalling up every 24 hours on a chart which, together with a pen on a string, was fastened to the kitchen door. It all worked out more or less until the day she pulled out her naso-gastric tube. We tried to get by without it but Anne-Marie was falling behind her required intake and a trip to the hospital became inevitable.

Going to hospital with Anne-Marie always required additional strength. We had to be of semi-presentable appearance, to be organized as to what to take for her and for me, to be adaptable to new and often unpleasant situations and to be outside of our normal routines. I had to be strong for Anne-Marie and prepared to converse with nurses and doctors. There were times when I did not make it to hospital with her because I myself did not feel able for it. On this occasion, however, I asked Pat to go with her because I wanted him to experience something akin to Anne-Marie and my relationship, which had been forged by going through suffering together.

Upon their return I tried to feed Anne-Marie her usual bottle-feed before topping her up through her new tube, but she kept turning her head away with tightly closed lips when the bottle was approaching. Maybe her swallowing ability was affected by the new tube? I became convinced that the British Health Service naso-gastric tube was inferior to its German predecessor. Irritation was rising within me. The aim to increase the oral intake so that the tube would eventually be superfluous was slipping out of sight. We seemed to have taken a sizeable leap backwards.

The new tube became the root of all evil in my eyes. I was out of sorts with myself for letting Pat go with Anne-Marie, thinking that maybe if *I* had gone, they might have put a thinner tube in and all this trouble could have been avoided. I phoned Clark Clinic and was reassured that they thought they had put the thinnest available model in. Very graciously they invited us to come back any time to have it checked out again and changed if necessary. I also phoned the Heart Centre in Munich who sent us a new German tube which arrived after Anne-Marie had got accustomed to her British one and her oral intake had improved slightly. We held on to our new German tube in case it would be needed in the future.

Anne-Marie became more and more unsettled when tube feeding, until finally one night she screamed and kicked as we were feeding her by tube, so that I ended up walking up and down the corridor holding her in my arms and rocking her while Pat followed behind me, holding up the funnel with the milk. Thankfully, she settled again afterwards. We knew: Hospital in the morning.

They pulled up the tube and found it kinked and bloody at the end. The tube had been pushed in too far. It had been poking into her. There was no point in putting another tube into such a raw stomach.

Back in "our" sideward we had to try to manage feeding and giving her some medicines for her stomach lining orally. These were tough days, battling out a battle of wills: "I want no milk" versus "You have got to take some milk."

Sr. Alison's innovation and positive outlook certainly helped to keep up the spirits. Different types of suckers, different sizes of holes in them, different spoons, different temperatures, different positions, different amounts of Duocal, different formula milks, different food (we were now even starting to introduce spoon-feeds), different distractions... While all these were not particularly successful, at least at every stage there was the hope that things might change for the better.

During this admission I experienced particular closeness to Our Lord. Pat had brought in a Russian 1998 icon poster calendar which my father had sent me. It had an icon of Jesus in the middle and the days of the year printed underneath. I hung it up in our little side ward covering over a children's poster of a tough looking, grinning character inside a glass bubble flying upwards with a frightened looking cowboy holding on to him for dear life.

The icon of Our Lord was peace-giving and promoted prayer – i.e., conversation with Our Lord. This was fine and good and wholesome but got very surprising to me when I realised again what I should have known already, that Our Lord Jesus is involved with every aspect of our lives.

I was filling in an application form for a course which had excited me: An evening course, two nights a week, of Catholic *and* Protestant theology. I had taken great care over filling in all the details, giving account of what I had done with my life so far and was just putting the form into the envelope when I glanced over to the icon. As an after-thought I said to My Lord, "This is all right with you, isn't it?" never really expecting to get an answer. *"Why?"* was His immediate response. The best answer I could think of was: "To get to know you better", whereupon I heard Him say: "You know me already!" All that was left to do was to throw the filled-in form into the bin.

Also, one early morning, after giving Anne-Marie a little feed of milk, burping her and putting her down, I lay down again, too, looking forward to a little more sleep, only to hear My Lord telling me to change her nappy now. I was most surprised, and also a little reluctant as I had done the 'nose-to-nappy-test' and as she was peacefully settling over again. I thought this was very strange.

I went with my nose to the nappy again but could smell nothing untoward. I was going to lie down again, thinking this could not be right and that I was starting to go funny in the head when I was told the same thing again. I got up, abandoned the idea of getting that extra wee sleep and just set about changing her nappy without disturbing her too much.

I was awe-struck when I opened the nappy and found it absolutely full with a nearly odourless load of very soft stool. Certainly, if I had not changed it then, Anne-Marie would have developed a red and sore bottom. And, to complete the wonder, He threw in an extra wee sleep for both of us even after the nappy change! -Thank You for caring about every detail.

I do not remember an outstanding feeding breakthrough but eventually we got by well enough to be allowed home without a tube. From this time on, Anne-Marie had to take both milk and medicines by mouth. We were given syringes (without needles of course) to administer the medication. They were to be used, cleaned, sterilised and then re-used.

Feeding was a constant struggle. Ideally a feed should have taken no more than 20 minutes and there should have been a definite break between feeds yet at the same time we had to aim for a minimum intake per day and had only 24 hours to try to approximate this.

Eventually experience taught us that feeding was hard to re-start after a time gap and that we had to feed continuously to be hopeful of Anne-Marie taking anywhere near the required amount. All other things had to take a backseat, and within a very short time the household collapsed all around me.

We had to continue with a milk diet for the time being as Anne-Marie had developed a passionate dislike of all types of baby food. She would have been the happiest child on earth had living not required eating or drinking!

Anne-Marie caught a vomiting diarrhoea bug during this time and needed hospital admission to a ward for infectious diseases. We were in a side ward with restricted visiting (parents only), separated from the main ward by a little enclosed corridor.

What a struggle. Anne-Marie did not feel like drinking *anything* – let alone the prescribed dioralyte. The drip was a constant threat and our already hugely underweight little darling became very weak and started running a temperature. In order to give her bowels a rest she was not allowed any milk but was supposed to live on dioralyte her heart medicines and a children's paracetamol solution.

Unlike at home, the nurses now had the responsibility for administering the medicines, and we were dependent on their mercy of remembering us at the right times and/or of not disturbing Anne-Marie if she had fallen asleep. Thankfully, especially the more experienced nurses did not mind leaving me in charge of drawn-up syringes, so that Anne-Marie would not need to get disturbed unnecessarily.

Medicines were often not drawn up very accurately though, and being pernickety about things I believe to be important, even in the middle of a lot of making-do in lots of other areas, (e.g., of most aspects of house-holding) I was a bit of a pain to the nurses, sending them back with syringes which, once the air bubble(s) had been removed, were not filled up to the required level...

I was getting tired. Tired of trying to set things right, tired of being positive, tired of illness and tired of remembering the collapsed household at home. A ray of hope in form of a little advert I found in the Lutheran Magazine of Ireland which Pat had brought in among other post was most welcome. A German girl, Friederike, was looking for a family to be an au-pair for in Ireland.

Why not use the disability money we were getting for Anne-Marie in this way? I phoned her but she was not too keen on Belfast and kept her options open. That was fine. It was uplifting just to think of the possibility of it working out. (It *did* work out later and she *was* a wonderful help to us.)

Bit by bit first the vomiting and then the diarrhoea stopped and Anne-Marie was started on half milk, half water, and later on undiluted milk. Back at home Anne-Marie did quite well for a few days but then her appetite deteriorated with intakes not even reaching the 300 ml mark over 24 hours and she started to have loose bowels again. I knew I could not keep her at home for much longer.

Seemingly by chance (although I should know better than that), I heard of Sr. Briege McKenna coming to Belfast, to St Patrick's Church not far from us. She is a Catholic nun who, divinely healed of arthritis herself, received a call to be involved in the Christian Healing Ministry. She is the author of the book "Miracles Do Happen", describing her personal journey and experiences of numerous healings in answer to prayer. I was undecided between taking Anne-Marie straight to the hospital or taking her to Sr. Briege's healing service.

The idea of taking little Anne-Marie, underweight and ailing into a church full of sick people, did not appeal. I phoned up the organisers to enquire if it might be possible, under the circumstances, to arrange a one-off meeting with Sr. Briege either before or after the service. As it turned out, I was not the only one with such a bright idea! Yet on this occasion Sr.Briege had to limit her time to the healing service, and was not able to receive individuals for prayer.

We decided to take Anne-Marie to the service just as this would be about to start, to keep the danger of additional infections to a minimum. Pat, an expert at last-minute-but-still-just-in-time appearances, managed to drop us outside the church doors one minute before the service was due to begin. St Patrick's Church is big and was filled to overflowing.

With Anne-Marie in Andrea's pink and cosy baby-sleeping-bag I walked down the side of the church to the very front row. There were a couple of spaces in the front row with "reserved" signs on them. I stood beside them indecisively when an official-looking person appeared, removed the signs and said: "They are not going to come now." We ended up sitting in the very first row!

Sr. Briege and a number of priests entered from our side and walked past us. She nodded and smiled over to us. I found it hard to believe that she had smiled at *us*, out of all the people here, and looked around to see if she had maybe meant the people beside or behind us, but they seemed oblivious to her greeting. I wondered if maybe Our Lord Himself had mentioned us to her. (I knew from her book that she had a direct line to Him and spent a number of hours per day directly with Him.)

The healing service went underway with singing and experiences retold by Sr. Briege, as well as priestly words of wisdom. Sr. Briege was praying at the front of the church and encouraged the congregation to pray and to put their petitions in front of the Blessed Sacrament which was carried from row to row through the whole church. She urged us to pray to it as it is Jesus.

And so I did, as I had never done before. I forgot about all the people around me, falling on my knees as He came by, asking Our Lord Jesus from the depth of my being, tears streaming, to heal and have mercy on our, - on *His* little Anne-Marie. In turn, His Spirit touched me, giving me absolute freedom to praise Him afterwards, joining in the singing to my heart's content, in harmony and all.

When the service was over, Sr. Briege made her way to the packed church porch. There she had a lot of hands to shake and was doing it very quickly with an exceptionally radiant glow and a smile on her face. She was thanking people for coming, bidding them farewell, wishing all the best....but it was only to Anne-Marie that I heard her commit herself by saying: "I'll pray for you." I felt privileged and was filled with joy. It was evening time, dark and cold. We went home, still open to the idea of taking Anne-Marie back to the hospital.

But things changed. The very next 24-hour period Anne-Marie took 600 ml of milk and also had no more diarrhoea. - *600ml!* This was far more than she had *ever* taken in one day in her whole life. (400 ml had been an excellent achievement up to then.) It was wonderful to see and totally uplifting. Her intake even increased from this over the next week or so going up to 800 and more ml per 24-hour period. *Thank You, God!*

With this breakthrough, Anne-Marie also developed an interest in other foods. For a while she took fromage frais without resistance and was open to sampling what her brothers and sister were eating so long as nobody dared to mash it up for her. We all got a great surprise and a good laugh when she managed to lay hands on the lid of a ketchup bottle one day and was licking the inside of it with relish and dedication. *Now* we knew what she liked! No bland foods please! It was always wonderful if she actually enjoyed eating something, although she was totally inconsistent with her likes and dislikes. What she was partial to yesterday might never please her again.

She also had a phase where she would only open her mouth if quality entertainment and good company were provided. Keys or other interesting objects needed to suddenly appear. She would then take them in her own hands, and when they were heading for her mouth a skilled person could just slip the spoonful in her mouth as it opened to receive the keys or similar, fractionally before these arrived. This continued until she got wise to it and put a stop to it by knocking the spoon flying! If she was not unwell she was always cheerful, at times even mischievous, and always greatly interested in everything and everybody around her.

Whatever little bits of solids and semi-solids she might have eaten, her main food still continued to be baby milk and this was often very difficult to persuade her to take. For a while, minute splinters of chocolate worked. She enjoyed them, and they left her mouth feeling very sweet. She would then take some milk to alleviate this. This had become as a last-resort stand-by until she decided she did not like chocolate any more.

I was caught up with feeding around the clock, and time lost was impossible to make up. A week's groceries' shopping, for example, took me about an hour. So if I went shopping she fell back on her intake schedule Of course, if I wanted to go somewhere Pat was always willing to try to feed her, but especially during her earlier months Anne-Marie would usually take more for Mummy than for anyone else. ...Nonetheless, I still liked to go to my Wednesday night Lamb of God Community meeting whenever possible. It gave me spiritual sustenance and was a mid-week top-up to the normal Sunday morning contact with God and His people.

Exodus 17 v.10: "As long as Moses held up his hands, the Israelites were winning, but whenever he lowered his hands, the Amalekites were winning ..."

We certainly felt the benefit of many people's continued commitment to prayer. For the first year of her life Anne-Marie seemed to be something of a barometer for the amount of prayer going up for her. Every week people would ask how she was keeping and would fashion their prayers accordingly. If Anne-Marie was well for a week or two and accordingly people were slackening their prayers for her, she got ill again very quickly and her prayer-partners had to be alerted to resume their petitions for her which always helped. This was teaching all of us the value of constancy and perseverance in prayer and was a pertinent reminder of the serious intercessory-prayer-responsibility we all have.

I get the impression that Northern Ireland's position - if you allow me to draw this comparison - is similarly affected. Whenever people get together large-scale to storm heaven for peace - especially cross-denominationally - the politicians make progress. And when forward steps have been taken and the storming of heaven ebbs away, political progress comes to a halt or regresses… Yet, even with the knowledge of the importance of prayer, time and again my own prayer life is far from satisfactory. Lord have mercy!

Being frequent hospital users, Anne-Marie and I met up with Jade again, the little girl who had survived a house-fire, whom we had met in the ICU before our trip to Munich. Her Granny made contact with us when she heard that we were "in", too. It was wonderful to see Jade's incredible improvement: Her face, which had been crimson when I had last seen her, was looking almost normal now. From now on we visited her every time we were in hospital.

1 Samuel 12 v.23: "As for me, far be it from me that I should sin against the Lord by failing to pray for you."

Jade got to know us, too, and in her husky voice called out "Anne-Marie!"- a joyful shout of recognition - whenever we came to visit. One of her grannies informed me that Jade would only be transferred to a hospital nearer their home when she was able to walk again. Walking was as yet a big problem due to the contractions in her legs. Granny asked me to pray for Jade's walking, and I said I would.

Anne-Marie was discharged home that day and to my shame the promise I had given to Jade's Granny went out of my head completely. It was about the third day, just as I was standing by Anne-Marie's cot, vacantly gazing out of the window while she was drifting over to sleep, that it suddenly struck me that I had promised to pray for Jade. I made an about-turn and headed straight for the kitchen and stood face-to-face with my calendar Jesus-icon. Whatever I said to Him, apologetically, about forgetting to pray for Jade, I was absolutely stunned by His response. In a gentle and kind, yet authoritative tone of voice He said: "*I had been waiting for your prayers*"

- Strong yet tender, both rebuke and encouragement...

A Short Life

I carried Anne-Marie with me everywhere I went. I learnt to do most things one-handed while she learnt to hold on to me by wrapping her legs and arms around me. One day I had her on my arm facing over my shoulder when going by the kitchen door. As her arms were reaching out over my shoulder towards the icon of Our Lord Jesus on the door, I stopped to observe. There was a smile of recognition on Anne-Marie's face. She was in inner conversation with Our Lord. After standing by the door for a while I explained that it was an icon of Jesus. She repeated after me: –"Sesus". She liked mentioning his name and in this way 'Sesus' became her first word in preference to 'Mummy' or 'Daddy'.

Anne-Marie loved all our icons. Going around the icons in our house on my arm at bedtime, she would entrust herself to the holy people depicted on them, often resting her head on the icons as we went around them.

Before she learned to walk, Anne-Marie developed the most unusual way of propelling herself forward. She would stretch one of her legs out to the side and push herself over it, ending up on her bottom and facing in the opposite direction to where she was trying to go. After a while she adjusted this and 'crawled' on all threes - with one little leg stretched out to the side.

We were expecting things to get easier from the one-year mark, as this had generally been mentioned as a landmark after which things *should* get easier. In Anne-Marie's case it took an extra month or two before we came to a more stable stretch with fewer hospital admissions. It was also around this time that she became confident on her own two feet, and as such unstoppable.

Her churching experience in autumn 1998 was an occasion, at which she was simply radiant. With a hand-full of faithful well-wishers in attendance, Fr Colm McBride (no relation) conducted the little christening ceremony in St. Therese's Church, our local Catholic chapel here. Again and again Anne-Marie longingly stretched up her little arms towards the cross which hangs towards the front of the centre aisle. It is a wooden cross carrying an icon-style image of Our Lord.

This did not seem to be in conflict for her with the fact that she was also irreverently "blowing raspberries" at the celebrant, thus causing quite a few chuckles among her siblings. Her grandparents from Germany had come over for the occasion and saw her in full flight, high-spirited, vivacious, cheerful, fully aware of being the centre of attention and lapping it all up.

Sharon, our friend and neighbour, had helped in the preparations and had given Anne-Marie her own christening gown to wear. Due to Anne-Marie's pitiful size it fitted her perfectly and looked like something of a ball-gown on her. Anne-Marie wore it as if there was no question about the fact, that she was, and always had been, a princess.

At a sit-down fish supper afterwards my parents witnessed Anne-Marie, this slight, fragile and pale looking little elf-like child, behaving like a ruddy-cheeked lover of the fullness of life, not only waving her chips about at the head of the table, but actually also happily joining into the eating! It was wonderful to see that the times of just one pea at a time had definitely come to an end and I was grateful for the new image of Anne-Marie which they would carry home with them.

Matthew 6 v.33: "Seek ye first the kingdom of God and His righteousness, and all these things shall be given onto you"

Many blessings came our way. As Anne-Marie was entitled to Disability Benefit and I was entitled to a small regular sum of money for carer's support, our weekly budget was increased by over fifty pounds a week. In our case, this made a *huge* difference and was most welcome.

Apart from statutory benefits, people seemed to be extra generous towards us as well and quite a few remarkable 'coincidences' happened, keeping me aware that our every need was being attended to meticulously. Things seemed to happen according to a pattern of three recurrent steps: First a perceived need in my mind, then an attempt at looking into ways of satisfying this need, and finally provision - for absolutely free. The three steps were making me appreciative. Had I not first felt the need, I may well not have appreciated the gift as much. Three examples spring to mind, although there literally are countless more:

When I was pregnant with Anne-Marie I had got it into my mind, that I wanted this child, who had such a special story, to have a swinging cradle. I had made enquiries, checked in shops and catalogues and started paying a deposit on one in a local shop, only to be given a beautiful old one free, by a prayer-group lady.

Our Papa's little folding bicycle, which he used to get to and from work when he was not jogging, was falling apart, and I wanted to get him another bike for his birthday. I checked in the catalogues and had nearly decided to order him one, which would have been paid off over so many weeks, when our friend and neighbour Monika told me without knowing anything about my plans that she had been clearing out her house and came across this bicycle which she had won in some competition and never used. Would we like it?

Anne-Marie seemed set to stay with us for a while (I had finally started buying double packs of nappies) and so I thought she should have her own little wardrobe, too. I needed storage facilities for sheets and bedclothes as well and was looking for wardrobes when Sharon called at our house, again unaware of my intentions, and reported that her husband's uncle had died, and there were two wardrobes left in his house, which they had to remove from it. Did we want them?

In similar ways we were given a settee, a number of working family cars as well as carpets, clothes and gifts of money, just exactly when they were most needed. At the time, I put these things down to the fact that I was a conscientious "tither", giving the tenth of every bit of money that came through my hands back to God through various charitable organisations, but now I feel that Anne-Marie's physical presence with us played an important part in attracting God's Grace and Mercy for our family.

During Anne-Marie's time on earth, I also received extraordinary spiritual blessings. I had only been listening semi-attentively when Anne-Marie's godmother Barbara talked about a retreat to be given by a group of Italians in the nearby St.Clement's Retreat House, until she remarked that this group was called "John the Baptist Community" (Koinonia Giovanni Batista[11]). Hearing *St. John the Baptist's* name mentioned was electrifying to me. Ever since Anne-Marie's conception story I had wanted to get closer to this great Saint, Prophet and Forerunner of Our Lord. Surely a community called after him would shed some more light on him for me!

Noticing my excitement, Barbara tried to say that the course was already fully booked, but I hardly heard her. I phoned various people and yes, as I lived near by and did not require lodgings for the weekend I got a place, not even knowing the theme of the course.

Matthew 3 v.11: "I baptise you with water for repentance but after me will come One who is more powerful than I, whose sandals I am not fit to carry. He will baptize you with the Holy Spirit and with fire"

The course, held in June 1999, turned out to be called "Baptism by Fire." It was not an academic discourse about the topic. Instead it was designed to facilitate a personal *experience* of baptism by fire. It was essentially the Pentecostal experience of the fire of the Holy Spirit of the Love of God, coming with such intensity that impurities had no chance of survival in His presence. This weekend had a most profound effect on me. Without a doubt I left a different person, to the one I had been when I arrived.

The consuming fire of the Spirit of God had done a big clean-up job and a great number of my impurities were burned up in it. All my catalogues went into the bin upon my return, as I did not want to be tempted to buy on credit any more and my competition craze had ended. Would not God provide for everything without me needing to concern myself with any of it?

I had come through an experience of God's love beyond the realm of this book and had experienced a physical healing. My feet were planted on the Rock of Ages and I had received a new freedom to believe and to work for evangelisation. I was no longer wasting time – at least not for the next number of months.

As if to certify the authenticity of what had happened by the raging of the evil one, bad news struck immediately after the course had finished. One of Pat's brothers died suddenly and tragically.

It was a pertinent reminder, that there are spiritual powers at work against which we as people are utterly powerless and that we all are dependent on the protection of Our Lord. It brought to mind the death of 21 Palestinians by the Wailing Wall on 8 October 1990 at the very hour we were getting married a short distance from there, in the church of St. Saviour in the old City of Jerusalem.

This in turn raised my awareness to the insistent necessity to cover each other in prayer, as well as to the hard-to-understand and hugely uncomfortable truth of the words of Isaiah 43 v. 4: *"Since you are precious and honoured in my sight and because I love you, I will give men in exchange for you and people in exchange for your life."*

1999 was definitely Anne-Marie's best year. It was also the first time we went on a foreign holiday with the whole family. This was due to the fact that a charitable organisation, the Family Fund Trust, gave out grants to families with seriously disabled children specifically and exclusively for them to go on holidays.

We had already benefited from one such grant in the summer of the previous year, when we had had one week in a holiday cottage at the North coast of Northern Ireland. This experience had raised my awareness to the fact, that it *was* possible to go on holidays with a child like Anne-Marie and had also nearly shocked me into realising there were other places on this earth apart from our four walls and the hospital.

Encouraged by this and by the fact that Anne-Marie's condition seemed to be a bit more stable and supported by many people's prayers for her health, we booked a week's family holiday in La Pineda, on the East coast of Spain, just south of Barcelona, which turned out to be a wonderful highlight of Anne-Marie's life.

With a climate which gave her full freedom to run around with as few clothes as she liked, with a pool with a children's section just immediately outside the enclosure of our veranda and a broad sandy beach no further than a five minutes walk away, this was the perfect place for Anne-Marie. Her calls of: *"Me pool!!"* still echo happily in all of our memories today. Had she had *her* way, she would have spent day and night playing in the pool.

It was also a family and friends' get-together, as my sister and her family had booked their holiday from Germany for the same holiday complex (Estival Park), and Reyes, Alma's Spanish godmother from Zaragoza came to visit us, too. She invited us home to her family (requiring a substantial inland motorway drive along dry Spanish countryside in my sister's people-mover) to the biggest royal welcome anybody had ever given any of us in our entire lives.

Her mother had worked until the early hours of the morning to prepare a more than five course meal for all of us, and everybody - the father, mother, granny (R.I.P.), Reyes and her sister - all had wrapped presents for all the children!! It was like Christmas and has become engraved in our memory as an overwhelming experience of love and hospitality lavished upon us.

Life beyond the year-and-a-bit mark rolled along quite well, with few exceptions. On one occasion Anne-Marie started to be grunty again. She had not been like this for such a long time that I had forgotten how distressing it is to witness. It was evening time and Anne-Marie was tired. I had to decide whether to keep her at home or to take her into the hospital.

I put her in her cot and measured her respirations. My watch with nightlight facility and second-hand had not been used like this for quite some time. She was not breathing faster than normal. She did not feel hot or sweaty to the touch. Knowing only too well that a trip to the hospital would mean a great lack of sleep for Anne-Marie and hoping that sleep would help her, I decided to monitor the development at home.

She went to sleep grunting with every breath. Inwardly I fell on my knees. All my inner composure had collapsed in an instant. I was pleading for mercy; I was beseeching my Lord to have mercy.

I lay down beside her cot and listened to her every breath. What was the cause of this? How would it progress? She appeared to be sleeping peacefully even in the middle of all the grunting. Time seemed to be standing still while my mind was churning over the possibilities and implications. Somehow, however, drowsiness settled on me eventually and I fell asleep.

Acts 16 v.25, 26: "About midnight Paul and Silas were praying and singing hymns to God, and the other prisoners were listening to them. Suddenly there was such a violent earthquake, that the foundations of the prison were shaken. At once the prison doors flew open, and everybody's chains came loose."

I dreamt that there was something like a haze, a fog, covering the land. People seemed to speak and relate to each other through this haze. It seemed to be the norm. Nobody remarked about it particularly, but it felt to me as though it was limiting us, as though there was great potential unrecognised and uncared for, as though *something* should happen to change the status quo. I started to sing praises to God and all of a sudden there was a force at work through me that I had no control over.

Like the water jets powering forth out of water-hydrants in summertime, when children open the fire-points to get soaked in the torrents of water gushing out to great height, so my praise swelled and burst forth in an unrestrainable flow. From the depth of my chest, up through the airways and out of my mouth it rushed with such power that my head had tilted backwards. It continued for quite some time and when it finally subsided I saw that the fog had lifted and the air was clear and pure and fresh and there was great joy among the people.

The next morning Anne-Marie was well again.

Anne-Marie was becoming stronger all the time. She had her own ideas and great willpower and was sometimes challenging to be with. She developed into quite a character. Being very perceptive, she loved impersonating people, especially Alma. If Alma was upset, Anne-Marie copied her behaviour in hilarious fashion. She would cross her little arms tightly in front of her chest, lower her head and stomp about proclaiming, *"Alma huff!"* She also imitated her brothers. When they had fallen out with our Papa over something, she ran into the kitchen, shouted at him as crossly as she possibly could and then waltzed off with a smirk on her face.

Her sense of humour was also appreciated by one of the nurses during a hospital admission when Anne-Marie had had a fever, but ice-cold feet. This nurse had got her some boy's socks to warm up her feet. Much to the amusement of the nurse and in spite of her fever Anne-Marie hopped off the bed and put on a "funny walk", for the benefit of the nurse, in order to show off these new socks to best effect.

Anne-Marie was very quick at solving problems. If, for example, I was not going to make chips for dinner because there were no chips in the freezer, she would insist: *"Get some then!"* This, or depending on the item in question, its counterpart *"Get one then!"* continues to be quoted among the members of our family.

Papa likes to remember her frequently repeated attempt at postponing bedtime: "No sleeps yet!" and her delight at the visits of auntie Fidelma, who came to type the beginnings of this book.

(I started writing this book long before Anne-Marie's passing.)
After her usual siesta, Anne-Marie would stand up in her cot
excitedly asking, if Auntie "Deml" had come.

Although occasionally her very strong character also
wearied me, it was probably more my exhaustion and frustration
of only ever dealing with the foam on top of the tidal-wave of our
permanent household mess that led me to let out a sigh to Our
Lord one day, as I was hanging up the washing in the bathroom:
"Oh Lord, how long?" To my surprise I heard a clear answer: *"Not
long now."* Yes, there was some relief in hearing this answer but
there was also an unsettling recognition of my own ungratefulness
calling for repentance.

*Galatians 6 v. 2: "Carry each others burdens, and in this way you will
fulfil the law of Christ."*

Anne-Marie had an unusually strong spiritual side to her.
One day I was quizzing Raphael, Pascal and Alma about who had
been responsible for some unfortunate incident. Each was trying
to blame the other and we were getting nowhere fast. Anne-Marie
had been upstairs and could not have caused the problem but, on
realizing her siblings' predicament, she made her way down the
stairs on her bottom, announcing half-way down *"My fault!"* - A
meditation on Christianity alive.

If ever she found me tearful, (for example when I read
some of the literature various charities would send to us) she
would run immediately to get a tissue to wipe away my tears. Also,

when she had heard that my sister's daughter Kerstin, whom Anne-Marie had met in Spain, was unwell, I was surprised to find her upstairs kneeling by the side of a mattress on the floor, hands folded, and head resting on them and on the mattress, deep in prayer.

Another time I found her quietly sitting on the landing with our biggest bible opened on her lap, with prayerfully folded hands, and that meditative, spiritual look on her face. I had come upon her during her bible meditation. This time I hurried down to get a camera.

Anne-Marie also had a courteous side to her, saying *"hank 'ou"*, after getting her nappy changed or after having her hair brushed or combed. If and when she was well, there was a balance between her strong willpower, courtesy, mischief, holiness and simple and pure fun, such as when she amused everybody including herself trying to walk in Uncle Brendan's heavy work shoes.

Any visitors she liked had to enter into play with her. She would stand in front of the front door as they were about to leave, stretching her little arms across it, making it impossible for them to leave without either playing with her, or else unceremoniously lifting her out of the road, a thing she did not appreciate.

Anne-Marie, although well most of the time now, still had episodes of sickness. On occasions she would have "morning sickness" and was extremely delicate. A wrong lift, position or suggestion etc., would make her vomit. If she started the day like this, it typically continued with bile when there was nothing else left in her stomach, and she looked very sick, pale and exhausted. Usually she was fine again after her midday sleep, although from time to time she had longer stretches of vomiting and needed to be nursed back to being able to keep things down by giving her a few millilitres of specially prepared liquid via syringe every few minutes all day long while carrying her about in an upright position.

During this period of her life I unexpectedly heard of the arrival of a young Orthodox Deacon and his wife in Northern Ireland. This was encouraging news and I made contact and was delighted to be one of the first members of an Orthodox mission in Belfast, benefiting from Readers Services and teaching sessions. When I joyfully shared this news with the late leader of the Focolare Movement in Ireland, Lieta, she simply smiled, saying "see how God loves you!"

One afternoon I received a phone-call from a mother I had met in Munich. After chatting for a while she said that she was not sure, whether it was on a trial basis, or whether it was to be a permanent change but the last time they had gone to the hospital, visiting times had been changed to twenty-four hour access to the children.(!) And although this was *fantastic* news to me, I was reluctant to research the details for quite some time, just in case things had reverted back to the restrictions.

It was not until a few years later, the day before what would-have-been Anne-Marie's sixth birthday, that I phoned up the hospital in Munich and got to speak to a very nice young receptionist. I enquired about parental visiting times, and she explained to me that *of course* parents would be allowed to be with their children 24 hours a day, both in intensive care as well as on the normal wards.

My chest was ready to explode with joy. I was unable to respond, and so she continued on, I had to understand that some very young infants were still being breast-fed and that it would not be right to restrict this through limited visiting times. When I put the receiver down I called out "Papa!" I wanted to hug somebody. *Instantly* the phone rang. It was Papa, just phoning from work. He said, "Hmm, she's been working quite hard behind the scenes, hasn't she?!"

I knew Anne-Marie loved animals, and wanting to give her as full a life as possible during her time with us, I had thought for some time that it would be nice to have a dog when a snap decision situation arose... Pat was *definitely not* for a dog inside our house and so the lovely black bitch which I had saved from going to the dog warden while waiting for the return of the schoolbus had to live in our porch.

We took Lassie for morning and evening walks every day, and when Anne-Marie was well enough she loved these visits to the park, exclaiming "Me loves Glassie!" For some reason she preferred calling her "Glassie". It was lovely to have such a nice dog, always happy to see you, but I felt for her having to live in the porch and thought about finding her a better home where she would be welcome to share the house.

Anne-Marie had been well until autumn 1999 when her pig's heart-valve began to leak, and even though medication could compensate for this to some degree she was greatly unsettled for days and weeks, causing her to behave like a headless chicken, unable to settle down to play and running around restlessly. The only thing that seemed to help to settle her was to strap her into her buggy and go for walks with Glassie.

We were in the middle of one of those walks in the nearby Grove Park when I suddenly remembered that Fr. Jim Burke from America, who was visiting the Lamb of God Community, was to celebrate Mass that afternoon. We marched from the park straight to the Convent on the Cliftonville Road, which in my walking terms is quite some distance, and arrived (by appointment) precisely on time. Anne-Marie settled down more or less for a large part of the Mass while Glassie was barking for us outside.

Fr. Jim is a lovely man, full of the love of God and with the most kindly expression on his face. He is a tall and elderly man. He was in the middle of celebrating Mass, when Anne-Marie took it upon herself to make her way to the altar. He noticed her and stopped all he was doing to stoop down from his height to this tiny little girl. He stooped down to her, put one of his big old hands on her front and the other one on her back, covering nearly her whole body with them, and stayed in this position for quite some time. The words: "She has come for some healing", are engraved on my mind.

I had got out of my seat as well, in order to retrieve Anne-Marie, and so was crouching next to her while Fr. Jim was praying with her. The Peace of the Lord was flowing through this man and I ended up covered in tears; tears of release of tension, tears of recognition of the Lord's Spirit of Love, tears of gratitude to this man, who was dropping everything to minister healing to Anne-Marie, and to God who was so tangibly at work. After this Mass Anne-Marie was no longer restless and continued being completely well for a further two months.

We had had Glassie for quite some time when I heard of someone who wanted to give a dog a loving home. We arranged that we could still take her for walks and left her with him. He gave me a pastel green fleece jumper as a sign of his thankfulness. I had not said bye-bye properly to Glassie, but thought, I would call again to see her the following day.

Driving up to see her the following day, I saw a dog looking just like her crossing the road and remember remarking to myself that if I didn't know I had left her with her new owner I would think it was her. Once I reached his house he told me that she had bolted on him. She had shot out the backdoor as he was putting the rubbish out, without wearing her collar and tag which would have identified her as my dog. A prolonged time of searching and putting adverts in local shops followed, but Glassie was never found.

All this happened not long before Anne-Marie's operation in Birmingham and I was painfully aware that it was trying to teach me something. It was not until after my return from Birmingham that I could see the parallels, in that I had seen Glassie for a short moment after having given her away only to then never see her again, just as I had got Anne-Marie back from her catheter study for a short while only to then not see her alive again.

Matthew 1 v.19: "Joseph her husband was a righteous man"

That same autumn Anne-Marie developed a particular interest in, and liking for St. Joseph. It all started with a little song, which Alma had brought back from school in preparation for Christmas: *"Knock, knock, knock, it's Joseph at the door, have you any room for us to stay?"* followed by an invariable negative answer to his question.

Anne-Marie was not impressed by this, and swiftly made this little song far more welcoming. She sang: *"Knock, knock, knock, it's Joseph at the door. Have you any room for us to stay? – **Yes!** Come in Jophes!"* It was as if she was also throwing open the doors of her heart to welcome this humble father figure with all of her being.

I, too, became more aware of the quiet unassuming spiritual strength which is his and recognised it in the father figure in our house: Our Papa, who was, after all, also named after him, bearing the two names Patrick and Joseph, also never pushed himself into the foreground but was always there to support and to help even if largely unnoticed.

I wanted an icon of St Joseph to manifest his presence with us pictorially, and was given one on which Joseph is holding the boy Jesus on his arm. A statue in St. Gerard's Church near us, also portrayed St. Joseph holding the child Jesus. This statue resembled in its features our Papa holding Anne-Marie and became a well loved representation of St. Joseph's gentle caring presence. It was as if St Joseph was taking over from St. John the Forerunner.

I wanted to take a photograph of this statue of St. Joseph with us to Anne-Marie's operation in Birmingham and asked a local photographer to take one. A friend gave us a lift to pick up the prints. When she gave them to Anne-Marie to hold she was absolutely astounded to see Anne-Marie's reaction. Anne-Marie excitedly exclaimed "St. Joseph! St. Joseph! St. Joseph!" over and over in absolute delight. This was *her* St. Joseph, and she kept on looking at him attentively, gratefully, lovingly and with such great joy. - In retrospect I am thankful that I had been blissfully unaware of the fact that, within the Catholic setting, St. Joseph is a Saint who is invoked when praying for a happy death.

188

It was quite something to face up to the fact that another operation was becoming inevitable so quickly and I wanted to make sure that we were going to the best possible hands. Our new Lutheran Minister told me of his friend who was a paediatric cardiac surgeon in Oslo, Norway. His friend talked to me at length over the telephone about what might be the best option for Anne-Marie. He pointed to the Children's Hospital Birmingham as having one of the very best paediatric heart surgeons in Europe, Mr. Bruin. He himself had worked with Mr. Bruin and was full of praise for him. However, towards the end of our conversation he conceded that not everything is possible only through human skill and technology.

I would not have had any hesitation about going back to Munich, even though at that time I was not sure of their visiting times, but I had heard that Professor Meisner had retired. Also, if there *was* an excellent surgeon available within the British National Health Service, it would save all the organisational hassle so long as the doctors in Belfast supported the idea of sending us across the water to England.

At the turn of the years from 1999 to 2000 Anne-Marie got ill. She was ill enough to bring her whole family into the waiting room of the casualty department in the Children's Hospital. She had a high temperature and was beside herself crying, holding on to mummy, nearly impossible to pacify and continued getting worse. With her eyes closed, all she wanted was to be carried about. As soon as I sat down, she got very distressed. Eventually Pat went to see if he could find a shop which would sell dummies as we had left hers at home.

We really only wanted to have her heart checked out to be sure that what she was suffering from was not anything related her heart-problems, and that it was o.k. for us to take her back home again. She was admitted, but released again later that day, as there were children suffering from bronchiolitis on her ward, and I was not too keen for her to catch bronchiolitis again after having had a harrowing time with her *suffering* from it the previous Christmas.

We went back home again and I began to think that we should go to Birmingham. They had such a well reputed cardiac department that they could surely also help her now. She had already been referred anyway so they would have some information on her there and if we came as an emergency they could not send us away again. Also, my friend Marge from nearby Wolverhampton would be only too willing to help with any unforeseen problems.

Anne-Marie was unsettled all night and I had to sit upright with her on my arm. I used the time phoning friends in America and making enquiries as to how best to get to Birmingham with a sick baby. By the time the morning was approaching I had reserved a flight for the next day for the two of us. Pat had helped to pack the essentials. We were ready to set off to the airport.

Coat on and bag in hand I decided by way of an afterthought on courtesy that I would give a quick ring to the

Children's Hospital in Birmingham to let them know that we were coming. I got to speak to a cardiac specialist who said that Anne-Marie did not sound well enough to travel. He strongly advised to wait until she was better and then to come over as arranged between the two hospitals.

Having made this call I could now no longer go ahead with my original plan, as that would have then been overtly disrespectful of his advice. So much for courtesy! What reassured me was that everything was probably going according to plan in the bigger scheme of things, was that Anne-Marie started to noticeably recover from the moment I decided to stay at home. Rehearsal only. Her time had not yet come.

To everyone's surprise, Anne-Marie requested to be given the "Falls Road dummy" when she had recovered sufficiently to speak with us again. Even in her state of sickness in the casualty department, she had heard and taken note, that Pat told us the story of how he had got the new dummy for her on the Falls Road!

Always checking the post with apprehension while waiting for a definite date for Anne-Marie's second operation, the weeks passed. I was feeling both anxious to go and anxious not to go to Birmingham. When the letter finally arrived, it gave dates and an outline of options which would be available to the team. It read very easily, but as I had finished reading, the whole experience of intensive care came flooding back, and even though I had always received strength from above the thought of it made me weak in the knees.

There and then, letter in hand, I fell on the kitchen floor in prayer to seek my God. On my knees, with my head on the floor I sought him. I sought reassurance that this was all in His will and that He was in charge. Little by little I received his Peace and experienced being led to understand that everything is happening according to His plan and that my part in it was being carried by Him and that I did not need to worry. I was inwardly reassured and got up again slowly after a while, able to continue with things in hand as though everything was quite normal.

One day I was sitting on the settee with Anne-Marie. She was peacefully resting her head on my lap. We were enjoying each others company without any haste. After a while Anne-Marie looked up at me and said, deliberately and peacefully, affirming, yet also searching my soul with her eyes: "...Operation, mummy." She knew within the depth of her being. She was just making sure that I knew, too.

The last two Wednesdays before our departure to Birmingham I was asked for the first time to lead the praise at the Lamb of God Community meetings. This was noteworthy to me. It was as if the time in the run-up to the operation became more and more praise-intensive.

Also in the then 'Siloam' Community where I went on Thursday evenings, I experienced the praise more powerfully than ever before. The Thursday before our departure, while immersed in praise with my arms and hands raised heavenward, an evermore increasing and free flow of fervent praise in unity with the community surged out of my heart and chest, through the open floodgate of my mouth. I felt something coming down from the heavenly realms. I did not know what it was but found myself gently guiding the unseen gift downward toward my right shoulder with both hands. Whatever it was came to remain on my right shoulder and had come leaving a gentle little smile on my face. I left it there, continuing with the praise.

Both the Siloam Community and the Lamb of God Community were aware of Anne-Marie's situation as outlined in the letter from Birmingham and had pledged their prayers for the following Tuesday's investigations under general anaesthetic, but particularly also for Thursday, the proposed day for her operation if her situation was deemed serious enough to warrant an immediate operation.

Shortly before our trip to Birmingham I also contacted our local priest Fr. McBride, and asked him to bless Anne-Marie before her big op. He came and experienced her healthy-enough looking little self, joining into bits of the "Our Father", which she was acquainted with, and playing a touch of peek-a-boo with him, hiding and reappearing from behind mummy's legs. I also informed him of the options and dates for the forthcoming operation. It was good to be assured also of his prayers.

Birmingham

The day of departure came and with it came farewells.

The children were to go to school as usual, so on one level it was a fairly normal, hectic, "get your uniform on!" type of morning. On another level, in order to ensure that Anne-Marie had the best possible chance to be well rested for all that lay ahead, I endeavoured to keep the noise to a minimum. Unfortunately I was not at all relaxed about this, which did not help the atmosphere in the house. Despite my best efforts, Anne-Marie wakened quite early.

Before leaving for school everyone gave Anne-Marie a little hug and kiss. When Raphael's turn came, he sat on the stairs holding her and did not want to let go. He looked serious and sombre. He had to be parted from her more or less forcibly and sent on his way to catch the school bus. It was not long before we ourselves had to set off, too. Things were moving at their own speed. We had become numbed carriers-out of the laid-out plans.

Just as we left the house ready to get into the car, Sharon was walking by. There was another farewell. She more or less jokingly suggested that she would keep Anne-Marie instead of letting her go to Birmingham. To my utter surprise I instantly felt a tough wall arising within me which did not allow me to enter into her joking suggestion on any level whatsoever. Up to that point I had not been aware of the strength of my inner conviction that we *had to* go. Things had to be met face-on now and there was no more room for frills.

I'm not a person for emotional farewells or for holding-on to the last second but that day it was difficult for me to let go of Pat. Quite atypically I found there were some tears rolling down my cheeks as we were checking-in the suitcase. I do not know if Pat saw them but he noticed that I was not quite ready to be parted from him and while keeping in mind the price of the parking ticket, he came to sit down with us again for a little while.

Anne-Marie was in great form. She was full of life and healthy-looking. She had no apprehension with regards to the journey in front of us and took everything in her stride. We had been issued with first class tickets which gave us access to the VIP lounge. To have a toddler in the lounge designed for business-people was unusual but Anne-Marie made herself at home without hesitation. Somebody gave her a packet of colouring-in pencils, some baked snacks and a drink of water.

In the first-class section of the plane were two wide black leather seats to a row rather than the normal three with fabric upholstery. I had seen the first class area of planes before but to be actually travelling in it was a new experience. For an instant the thought that this was maybe an unnecessary way of spending Health Service money came to mind but I quickly resolved to take pleasure in the journey instead of feeling guilty about it. It was to be enjoyed as an experience courtesy of Anne-Marie.

Anne-Marie was enjoying herself. She was busy with her colouring pens and keeping me in chat. The only thing that did not live up to her expectations was the flight experience itself. As she was looking out of the window of the plane she saw a uniformly light-blue sky. The flight was smooth and free from bumps or turbulences and so she suddenly came to a very firmly drawn conclusion. She proclaimed: "It's not moving, mummy; it's not moving!" No amount of careful explanation was going to change her opinion, as every time she looked out of the window she found her assessment of the situation confirmed. We just had to let that one go.

Arriving in Birmingham I was instantly reminded of my life in the English West Midlands when I had been so used to this wonderful conglomeration of peoples of different cultures and races living with each other much more peacefully than not. Here in the airport building people of all the different shades of skin colour mixed and mingled naturally. It was good and homely to breathe this freedom again.

We took a black taxi so that Anne-Marie could remain in her buggy in the centre-part of the cabin. It was the time for her all-important midday nap and I told her to close her eyes and to take a rest. Even though she was very chirpy and found everything interesting, to my surprise she actually closed her eyes for a while just to keep me happy. But after a little while she tested the waters by just opening one eye, or sometimes both, to look at something passing by, and then she closed them again as soon as I noticed.

The Birmingham Children's Hospital is a big building. Our ward was airy, light and new. We were assigned to a particular corner by a window with a cot, a chair and a little locker on which I placed St. John's icon. Later I also had the use of a folding bed for myself. A motherly-type nurse took our details and fitted Anne-Marie with an identity-armband. She also organised some chips and beans for us even though lunchtime had already come to an end on the ward.

Anne-Marie wanted to play and Dr. Simon, who was next in line to interview us, found us in the toy room. He was happy to let Anne-Marie play with a truck and other toys while writing his admissions report. Afterwards he stopped for an instant at our little corner and looked at the icon of John the Baptist before heading on his way.

Preparations for the following day had to be made. The next day, Tuesday, was the day for the catheter study as well as the examination of the heart from its back, through the oesophagus by means of a technique (transoesophageal echocardiogram) devised by Dr. Stümper, a German specialist in Birmingham.

To take some blood and in preparation for the next day Anne-Marie was to have a line put in her hand. This required a bit of "magic cream" to reduce the pain. Knowing how hard it had been in the past to get her veins, I was not looking forward to it. Dr. Simon and a very able young nurse awaited us in the treatment room. With Anne-Marie on my lap, I was holding her arm as they poked at her with a needle. Her veins were difficult to get. Magic cream or not, it was painful and sore and Anne-Marie was getting quite distressed. With a big bandage around her hand to secure the line we were sent off for an electrocardiogram on a different floor of the hospital.

Anne-Marie had barely recovered from the ordeal on the ward when she was now required to get undressed and have sticky pads stuck all over her and then sit totally still in order to get a good reading... The darling! She was afraid of these pads but after getting a number of them on she turned round to me, tears still in her eyes and said as though it had come as a perfect revelation to her: "They're not sore, mummy!"

I do not remember much about the echo-scan but the final thing she was subjected to was an x-ray of the chest. By this stage she was tired and clingy. She had had enough of strangers doing things with her which she neither wanted nor understood. And now she was supposed to take her clothes off again and sit in this artificial position with bits here and there and hold still. Anne-Marie was positioned for the x-rays when the radiographer asked me if I was pregnant. I said I could not be a 100 percent sure. She pointed out that in this case she would have to ring up to the ward and get a nurse to come down to hold Anne-Marie for the duration of the x-ray.

I thought of the delay, of Anne-Marie already undressed and distressed enough without being handled by yet another stranger. I could not bear the thought of all this. A quick thought up to God, I changed my tune. She left the decision up to me. I held Anne-Marie while wearing a lead-filled safety-garment against x-ray penetration. We were a good team and she needed me by this stage.

On the way back to the ward I thought we might try to find the chapel, as I was intending to spend the following morning there while Anne-Marie was to undergo the planned investigations. The Chapel for all Faiths had a prayerful feel to it. Anne-Marie on arm we entered reverently if a little intrigued as to what we might find behind the curtains in the segregated areas for men and for women. We entered the women's area and found prayer carpets on the floor all positioned in the same direction, presumably Mecca. I tried a little prayer to Our Lord kneeling on one of them, shoes off as prescribed.

Even though I am sure that He heard us no less from there than from anywhere else, it felt a little strange to think, that this might be my place and position for the following morning. How would it be if other ladies were going to use the chapel as well? Were the prayers going to be silent or sung? Having come to some level of acceptance of all that we found we headed out again to explore the hospital a little further.

A visibly worried and silently suffering mother shared the lift with us. At some stage she let out a deep sigh. She left the lift and as the elevator doors were closing I caught sight of the sign above the door behind which she disappeared: Intensive Care. That said it all.

Eventually we came upon the Christian Chapel. It came as something of a surprise as well as a bit of a relief. It felt hugely more familiar and much more comfortable than the previous one.

Prior to Tuesday's investigations we also met with Dr. Stümper. During our meeting it emerged that the medical team was planning to operate on Thursday. I listened to what he had to say. There was now no mention of first waiting for the results of Tuesday's two tests before planning further action. Indeed even the type of operation to be performed on Thursday had already been decided. Of the three options, which had been listed on the letter to us they had chosen the most difficult one.

Acts 8 v.32 & 33 (Quoting from Isaiah): "He was led like a sheep to the slaughter, and as a lamb before the shearer is silent, so he did not open his mouth."

The doctor's words to me had been: "It is our ambition to carry out *this* operation…." and like the lamb led to the slaughter I was unable to respond. I felt that *ambition* was probably not the right motivation to come to such an important decision but I was unable to respond, unable to think of ways of putting my thoughts across in a friendly and thoughtful way so that they could have been received. So his words were left standing, unquestioned, unchallenged. …Hopefully they knew what they were doing.

Remembering our experience in Munich where it had been decided to go ahead with the operation without putting Anne-Marie through the strains and stresses of catheterisation prior to operating and in view of the fact that the medical minds in Birmingham were already made up as to which operation to perform, I wonder in retrospect if the planned pre-operative investigations were strictly speaking necessary.

Evening came and with our curtain drawn around our little corner, we tried to sleep as best we could. I was very aware that Anne-Marie had had a strenuous and tiring day and that she had missed out on her hours of noontime napping. If Anne-Marie was to be in top form for the morning, she needed all the sleep she could get. But she was a naturally light sleeper and a naturally interested person. We both lay down after having had some light supper. She was then not allowed to eat anything more and her last drinks had also to be taken by a certain time in preparation for the general anaesthetic the following morning.

Neither one of us had a particularly restful night. I heard her every move and she was alert to every sound on the ward, following the nurses' footsteps with her eyes as they walked past our curtain.

Isaiah 53 v.10: "Yet it was the Lord's will to crush him and cause him to suffer..."

On Tuesday morning she was not allowed anything to eat or drink. Anne-Marie, the child who had had to be coaxed into eating, was asking for food and drink without success. Even with careful explanation it remained incomprehensible to Anne-Marie that Mummy would not let her have anything to eat or drink. To make matters worse there was a delay in getting the procedures started. Mummy tried as best she could to pull out all the stops to keep distractions going and to defer the hunger-pangs until later. Anne-Marie and I paid a visit to the play room where she made a little biro drawing, explaining that the squiggles on the paper were penguins.

Eventually we were called and a nurse accompanied us to the operating theatre. In a room adjacent to one of the theatres a very nice lady anaesthetist was waiting in readiness for Anne-Marie. I was allowed to hold Anne-Marie while she administered the anaesthetic which acted much more quickly than I had anticipated. To see Anne-Marie fully knocked out within a flash was something I had not been prepared for. I lent down to her and gave her a little kiss saying: "God loves you!"

I had wanted to give her the best I had and that to me was the knowledge that God loves her but after I had said it and was whisked out of the side-room, I felt I would have also wanted to say "Mummy loves you." It would have maybe sounded more personal, closer, more easily touchable…

A little tear appeared in my eye. The nurse walked down the corridor with me… I wiped it away. It was strange to have seen her lose consciousness so suddenly. The nurse looked across to me and I muttered something like that it had been my first time to see her getting anaesthetised.

I made my way to the chapel and started singing praises to God. I was determined to praise Him even though it was definitely not easy to keep the momentum going all by myself. I had brought a booklet with many praise songs and sang more and more of them but somehow never experienced the break-through to freedom, to the sure knowledge of being in the presence of God. At times I was a little self-conscious in case that someone else had wanted to use the chapel and I might put them off and at other times I had an eye on the clock. There seemed to be something of a heaviness upon me. My voice did not soar. It was watery and pitiful. Time was moving slowly.

Sometime after midday my sister arrived in the chapel, rucksack on her back, from Germany. I was glad to see her and went back to the ward with her. There were no immediate reports about Anne-Marie forthcoming. We were trying to sort out where Verena would stay when a nurse informed us that the procedures were now finished and that Anne-Marie was crying for her Mummy.

To my own disbelief I acknowledged what she had said without charging down the corridor at full speed to be with my little darling but finished another two or three sentences with my sister first. I was appalled at myself, although not acting on it. Never before had I experienced such detachment from the knowledge that Anne-Marie was crying.

Coming down the corridor towards the operating theatre I heard her crying and calling me. Finally my motherly instincts took over and I ran full of remorse and love and pity towards the sound of her voice into a large, nearly empty recovery room. Someone whom she did not know was trying to lift her bare- but for the nappy- body up on his arm totally against her wishes, apologising that he had not managed to calm her down.

We wrapped around each other. There were lines coming out of her everywhere. I did not count them. I ignored them. I wanted to be with my Anne-Marie, my darling, my precious, tortured, momentarily neglected, fragile and hurting treasure, my little one... Being more concerned to be reunited and reconciled with Anne-Marie I only half-heard when I was told that they had decided to leave the lines in place, as the operation was to be the following day instead of Thursday and that Mr. Bruin would speak to me about that later.

On our way back to the ward my attention was soon divided. There was Auntie Verena and there was the nurse who was pushing along a drip-stand with whatever they had decided to drip into Anne-Marie's body. Trying to be present to them both, I somewhat neglected to be also attentive to Anne-Marie on my arm.

When we arrived at our little corner where her cot and my camp bed were waiting for us it was early afternoon, Anne-Marie's usual nap-time. I thought that the best thing for her to do was to have a little sleep, to sleep off the effects of the anaesthetic and to gather up some strength for the operation on the following day and also because she had missed out on sleep during the night and day before. So I lifted her into her cot with all the lines coming out of her and told her to lie down.

How I was expecting her to behave as normal under the circumstances is now hard for me to fathom. It is true that in the past I had experienced how my treating unfamiliar circumstances as normal had helped her to do the same…but how I did not realize that this situation was so much more than 'unfamiliar' escapes me to this day and remains a source of humility for me. I am not perfect and Anne-Marie was the one who had to bear the consequences of this truth!

Psalm 69 v. 20: "I looked for sympathy but there was none, for comforters but I found none."

Anne-Marie tried to lie down in obedience but got up again unable to settle in any position when lying down. She called for me to lift her out of the cot. At home Anne-Marie would lie down and go to sleep if I was *not* in the room. So I thought that here, too, she might settle better if I was not disturbing her from getting her rest by being there. I told her to lie down and walked up the ward a little, talking to auntie Verena as we had not seen each other in a long time. Anne-Marie could not settle and Auntie Verena decided to leave to sort out where she would stay and to come back in the evening.

I seem to remember that Anne-Marie was allowed something light to eat which did not agree with her. At any rate, she got into her familiar highly sensitive vomiting pattern and was then restricted to liquid only. She was unquenchably thirsty and drank nearly a whole cup-full all in one go, only to vomit it all up again. From then on we had one heartbreaking struggle with restricting her liquid intake to small sips at regular intervals.

Anne-Marie was agitated in the cot as well as out of the cot. To my shame I must admit that it took me a very long time to understand that she was not only upset but also in pain with all those lines coming out of her. One line, entering in the groin, and internally continuing through her blood-vessels to her heart (as I understood it) must have been particularly unpleasant, while others were pulling at her or at the sticky plasters and/or bandages with which they had been secured to her body whether she moved or whether she kept still.

Once I *had* understood, it seemed to take an eternity before there was a nurse in sight who could be alerted to this, as we were slightly out of view in our little corner and a further eternity until she had got a doctor to prescribe a paracetamol suppository. In fact the nurse came back after a little while to enquire again if I really wanted to go ahead with it, as it would not be possible to give the paracetamol orally in view of the vomiting.

I was left wondering if 'they' did not think that she needed it, too. Had I not a fragile, restless, tired and clingy little girl on my lap on my camp-bed, holding on to mummy in a state of sickness and exhaustion unable to sleep due to pain and discomfort? In addition to all this she was also running a slight temperature.

I have a vague memory of my old friend Marge from Wolverhampton coming to visit us that day but being a sensitive and understanding mother herself, she did not stay long once she saw what state we were in.

It took me all my concentration and energy to be there for Anne-Marie, to try to reassure her, to hum to her, to sway gently from side-to- side with her. There was no way I could have left her in this state either by herself or with a stranger. My visit to the toilet had to wait.

Mr. Bruin came to speak to me. He pulled up a chair, and opened the conversation by asking me what I understood about Anne-Marie's condition. Why would he need me to tell him what he knew already? I muttered a few things of what I knew but feeling rather set upon I did not have all the correct terms to hand. Was he really expecting me to give him all the medical information I knew while I was struggling to be present to Anne-Marie?

His turn came and he had a lot to say. He spoke with eyes sparkling with intelligence and self-confidence. ... He would have carried out a different operation than the team in Munich... He had decided to operate tomorrow rather than Thursday because of the catheter study findings... (I thought very forcibly, and *nearly* said out loud: "But no-one will be praying for her tomorrow!" I had told everyone to be praying *on Thursday*!)

He informed me, that people with 'Anatomically Corrected Transposition of the Great Arteries' had not a long life expectancy and that therefore he not only wanted to perform a valve-replacement but also intended to 'switch around' those vessels adjoining the heart, which would then facilitate more normal heart-function for both the heart-lung and the systemic circulation.

It was obvious he had firmly decided which operation he wanted to perform. I was reminded of a little reflective thought Dr. Craig had expressed when he had said that going to Birmingham would open up more difficult choices but that he would be inclined to go with it if Mr. Bruin was to opt for even the most difficult operation mentioned in their letter. This was the one scheduled for the next morning. I did not oppose the flow of events.

Anne-Marie was not at all well. There she was, my poor little darling, exhausting herself vomiting up any little bit of liquid she had taken. Just as I was pondering the reasons for this, the anaesthetist of tomorrow's operation came to talk with me. I mentioned Anne-Marie being sick, quietly querying if something might have gone wrong during the procedures today.

He was not at all interested in exploring this idea and said without a flicker of compassion that the only reason for her vomiting was her heart-problem. Surprised at his coldness I asked him how then he would explain that she was apparently totally well and certainly not vomiting before we had come to Birmingham and added in a bout of despondency more to myself than to him that maybe we should not have come at all. He retorted in a fighting sort of spirit: "Maybe you shouldn't have! Why did you come anyway?" Aware that this sort of conversation was not leading anywhere good I tried to conciliate him, with no tangible results. Even now the outstanding and irremediable coldness of this meeting still dumbfounds me.

Another person who came to speak with me was one of the liaison officers. She was a bubbly and cheerful sort of person and offered to take me to have a look around the intensive care unit. I declined her invitation. She asked me if I had any questions and I admitted that I did. I asked her if she could find out if there was any way in which, in case of Anne-Marie's death, her remains could be brought home to Belfast without getting embalmed[11].

Asking this drew a silent tear or two from my eye. She advised me not to ask such questions at this stage but I persisted, explaining that I had also asked similar questions prior to Anne-Marie's first operation. She agreed to make enquiries and to let me know in the morning. She was one of two liaison officers working with this ward. Their names were female forms of Peter and Paul, thus bringing two powerful pillars of the Church to mind.

Verena had found somewhere to stay for one night and came back in the evening just as Anne-Marie's suppositories finally worked sufficiently to allow her to drift into a little bit of sleep. She was not sleeping soundly though. Every time I moved a little her hand would hold on to whatever part of my clothing it could reach to make sure I would stay with her but eventually I could make a much needed trip to the toilet.

Lights were dimmed and Anne-Marie was 'sleeping' on my camp-bed while I was hunched up at the foot-end of it. Night staff were under orders to check Anne-Marie's blood pressure and temperature every half hour. Of course they were only doing their job but it was not conducive to giving Anne-Marie that good sleep she needed.

Anne-Marie's blood pressure results were anything but spectacular. Sometimes they had to be repeatedly re-taken in the hope of getting a result that was within a more acceptable range. The pitifully pleading appeal to the nurses "Mummy do it!" still resounds within me. And indeed, Mummy turned nurse that night, putting on and off the blood pressure-cuffs and measuring the temperature every half hour. To start with Anne-Marie let her dislike of these investigations be known but little by little she relaxed more and more into the procedures, finally just letting them be done without any resistance.

She was allowed a little drop of water after every disturbance. It became like something of a ritual between us at the end of each of these sessions, for me to give her a little drink, for her to ask for more and for me to assure her that she would get more later. Hearing the assurance, she relaxed back into slumber for the next twenty minutes or so.

Her beautiful trust in Mummy was very moving and when on one occasion, just as she had laid back to go to sleep again, her little hand came to rest on mine, I felt such a flow of love streaming from it that I was inwardly warmed and filled with it. Her warm peaceful hand of love touched me lastingly.

1 Peter 1 v. 1 & 2: "To God's elect ... who have been chosen ... for obedience to Jesus Christ and sprinkling by his blood."

In the spiritually receptive drowsiness of the night I got the idea that it would be good if Anne-Marie were to be touched by the Blood of the Lord. She had never been allowed to partake of the Eucharist and had therefore never had the opportunity to be touched by His Blood in *this* way.

I felt an urgency about it which did not allow me to discard the thought. Remembering that I had received the Body and Blood of our Lord the day before coming to Birmingham I supposed that there should still be some of it flowing through my body. I reached for the corner of my suitcase which was underneath our folding-bed and pulled out my travel sewing kit.

Tentatively trying to pierce the tip of my right index-finger with the needle, I could not help thinking what a coward I was. There was Anne-Marie, full of holes and lines, into her groins, into her arms and all over, and here was I, too squeamish to give myself a little prick. The third attempt proved successful enough to draw a little drop of blood.

Ephesians 1 v. 13: "Having believed, you were marked in him with a seal, …"

Just as I lent forward and put this little drop on her forehead, someone (an Angel?) said: "Sealed by the Blood of the Lamb." It was reassuring to hear. It was confirmation of what I had been prompted to do. Although this left my rational mind far behind, I was contented I had done the right thing.

Ash Wednesday

Even after this night followed a morning, the most difficult morning in my life so far. The daylight and the day-staff greeted us. Anne-Marie was exceedingly thirsty. With all the curtains pulled back and the lights blazing there was now no more falling back to sleep between assessments.

There was also no more liquid allowed in the run up to the operation. Anne-Marie was running a temperature. I mentioned this to the staff, questioning if it was wise to go ahead with the operation under these circumstances. The nurse assured me she would mention it to the doctors.

Anne-Marie was desperately hungry and thirsty. Auntie Verena arrived and together we tried our very best to provide distraction. Reading from Anne-Marie's favourite 'Noddy' book worked until I foolishly read about Noddy and his friends having some buns. Anne-Marie was grief stricken that she did not have any. Having given up on Mummy she was now calling for Papa to give her a bun or something to eat or to drink, crying and wailing in hunger, thirst, discomfort, disbelief and alarm, totally unable to understand why nobody would give her anything.

Vaguely aware that St. John the Baptist's time as the preparer of the way may have come to an end, I felt that the time for Anne-Marie's beloved Saint Joseph had come. I thought that this gentle father-figure who had helped to raise Our Lord should be called upon to intercede, especially as Anne-Marie had such great love for him. Auntie Verena attached the photograph of the statue of St. Joseph with the child Jesus to St. John's icon which I had permission to bring to theatre, fastening a bible-verse between them: 'Nothing is impossible to God.'

John 19 v. 28: "...Jesus said, 'I am thirsty.'"

Time moved very slowly and Anne-Marie's thirst got worse. A delay in the op prolonged her agony. I kept trying to distract her and repeatedly promised that I would give her a drink later-on. Eventually we were called. I picked Anne-Marie up on my arm. A nurse dealt with all the lines and auntie Verena accompanied us. Walking down the corridor I was carrying *a little bundle of life*, a light little bundle of life on my arm.

Acts 6 v.15: "All...looked intently at Stephen and they saw that his face was like the face of an angel."

I carried my little bundle of life into the room where nurses and the anaesthetist were waiting for us. I sat Anne-Marie down on the table with my left arm around her little uncovered back and her side, staying close by her. The anaesthetic was to be given in two separate syringes. The first one was drawn up and given into a line on the back of one hand.

Immediately Anne-Marie started to chuckle and to laugh, looking upwards in front of her, radiant with happiness and delight. It was as if every pain and concern had dropped off her, as if she had complete freedom and total lightness and joy. She was looking at a specific place up in the air in front of her, chuckling, laughing, radiantly smiling.

It was an incredible moment. The nurses standing by were drawn into Anne-Marie's intense festive celebration of joy, release and blessedness, themselves enchanted and transfixed in looking at her, their own faces shining with love.

My sister had been watching through a window in the door. She could only see Anne-Marie's back, but had been captivated by the radiance of the faces of those looking at Anne-Marie. Her joyous heavenly smile and chuckles was reflected in their faces.

The second syringe followed all too quickly and instantly Anne-Marie was gone. I gently lowered her head onto the hard table, kissed her and whispered: "Mummy loves you" to her.

I now feel that this had been the moment when Anne-Marie was welcomed into the heavens by someone - maybe her beloved St Joseph - and that her Spirit had departed then, even before the operation.

I left, powerfully charged with the experience of this extraordinary event. All I wanted now was to make my way over to the chapel to start singing praises to God.

Job 1v.21:"Naked I came from my mother's womb and naked I shall depart. The Lord gave and the Lord has taken away; may the name of the Lord be praised."

Back on the ward a nurse compassionately enquired what we were going to do now. I was surprised at noticing an invisible inner steel barrier towards her compassion within me and answered that we were now going to the chapel to praise the Lord for bringing Anne-Marie through the op alive. Immediately when the words had left my lips I knew in my spirit that this was not correct. It was wrong. We were not going to praise Him for bringing her through the op alive. We were simply going to praise Him.

Verena and I went to the hospital chapel with the Lamb of God songbook and started singing the praise and worship songs from it. We continued, sometimes in unison, sometimes in harmony, singing praises and worshiping the Lord without ceasing until lunchtime when we made our way over to the Ash-Wednesday Service and Mass in nearby St. Chad's Cathedral, which was full of people. Receiving the blessed ashes onto our foreheads we were reminded of our transient life on earth. This was immediately followed by the Eucharist under both species, which was a wondrous blessing to me. Back in the hospital chapel we continued singing for hours.

In the late afternoon Dr. Stümper and Mr. Bruin walked into the Chapel together, looking concerned. They walked up to us and explained that the operation had been completed but that Anne-Marie's heart, once restarted, was not strong enough to keep up its pumping activity for any length of time. They had found that when restarted, it would pump for a little while before slowing up and then coming to a halt.

Before I knew what was happening and totally to my own amazement I heard myself speaking to them directly from my heart (as this was still open from all the praise) without the head even having *any* checking-function: "Don't worry," I said, "I have handed her over to the Lord."

Apparently they had restarted her heart twice with the same result. This was a lengthy process which each time involved raising her body temperature and then lowering it again for a rest period before the next attempt. Mr. Bruin was now explaining that there was one further thing he could try, but that to date it was reportedly not really successful in children. It involved trying to insert something like a balloon which was supposed to support the heartbeat.

With my head still largely out of action I found myself again responding from my heart, saying that if he was not too hopeful that it would help, not to put her through this. They took note and prepared to leave, saying that they would re-try to start Anne-Marie's heart one more time. Perhaps the rest it had had might have given it a chance to strengthen up.

Once they had left I was intending to continue with the praise but their words slowly began to sink in and I was beginning to have (second?) thoughts. How could I so calmly reject Anne-Marie's possibly only chance? I had to ring Pat, urgently, to get his view on the situation and maybe advise them differently. Back on the ward I rang and told him things were not looking good. I mentioned the option of inserting a balloon. He did not have any strong feelings or advice but he was supportive. I told him that all depended on this final re-start.

Inwardly somewhat restless now, I was unsure if I had made the right decision to reject the balloon option and wondered if I could reverse it. I spoke to a nurse who said they would surely try everything anyway. Short of going to the theatre myself there did not now seem to be a way to communicate with the doctors. The nurse also commended me for the courage of responding as I had and said that to be under the anaesthetic for too long often had lasting and damaging effects on brain function which could leave children mentally disabled.

Psalm 116 v.5: "...precious in the eyes of the Lord is the death of His saints..."

I requested that Anne-Marie should receive the sacramental Anointing of the Sick and the liaison officer set about arranging this. In due course a priest from the Cathedral arrived ready to perform this service. All was set to go ahead until he heard that Anne-Marie was in the operating theatre. For some reason he declared that under those circumstances he could not go ahead with the anointing. He pointed out that he had a churchful of people waiting for six p.m. Mass and Ashes and disappeared without further ado, leaving us puzzled and perplexed.

In answer to one of my questions the liaison officer mentioned the mortuary. I told her quite innocently that if Anne-Marie were to go there I would stay with her. When our helper pointed out that it was very cold down there I assured her that I did not mind this as I had brought a coat and a hat with me.

Our friend encouraged us to use the time to do some more praying, pointing out that if at all, Anne-Marie needed our prayers *now*, as things were still hanging in the balance but when questioned about the likelihood of Anne-Marie making it through, she conceded that there was not much hope. Verena and I decided to take up position outside the operating theatre to be closer to hand and to have another time of prayer there.

For a while I separated myself from Verena, entering into silence, bent forwards with my eyes closed, trying to inwardly encourage Anne-Marie to decide to stay with us; to stay with each one of us. I brought to mind her brothers and sister, her father and mother, who all loved her and wanted her to live with them so much but I did not feel that I was really getting through to her or that I had really dug deep enough to reach out from the centre of my heart which seemed to know that Anne-Marie's destiny was not to stay.

For a moment or two I regretted that I had not used the day for petition prayers to God; that I had not spent the day pleading for her life instead of praising Him. For a moment or two I felt I had let her down badly. There was the pain of feeling a failure as the mother of Anne-Marie, and then, as if to interrupt those thoughts, the two doctors came walking towards us out of the operating theatre.

They came together, Mr. Bruin and Dr. Stümper, up to where we were sitting. They told me that Anne-Marie had died. Mr. Bruin explained that he might have done the operation in two parts, one today and one tomorrow, with intensive care in between and I said, again from the heart that I was glad that he had not put Anne-Marie through this type of ordeal. He was grateful for my response.

He said another few things and mentioned that she might have come through the straight valve-replacement operation all right but that the long-term prognosis of repeated valve replacement operations with the other problems still unchanged would not have been good and that given the same circumstances he would opt again for the same operation he had done.

I thought this a little strange in view of the fact that Anne-Marie had died but let it go without comment at the time, thinking that maybe this was his way of coping with her death. It could also have been an attempt at minimising the risk of action taken against him, but I now think that his comments simply confirm that Anne-Marie had not died because he had chosen the wrong operation but because it had been her appointed time.

I changed the topic of conversation and said: "I want to be with her." Mr. Bruin said he could understand this and that he would be the same if it were his daughter. I wanted to go into the operating theatre with them. Dr Stümper did not mind but Mr. Bruin said they would bring her out to me, they would just tidy her up a bit and then, in five minutes or so, they would bring her out to me.

I went to the ward to ring Pat. - I got the answer phone and left a message: "Anne-Marie has died" – pause – This was the first time I had spoken those words, and they tried to choke me. I said another few things and then hung up.

Upon return I wanted to go straight into the operating theatre to be with her. What was there to be so secretive about? The anaesthetist emerged from somewhere and I asked him if Anne-Marie had done *anything* at all after the anaesthetic had been given, such as opening her eyes, or anything else. He was not for talking. He looked shifty, edging away, and said "No." The way in which he had answered left me unsure if he had spoken the truth.

They showed me into a rather large empty room off the main corridor, which was in semi-darkness, gave me a chair and brought Anne-Marie out to me, putting her into my arms. I called Verena, who had been waiting respectfully in the corridor, in to be with us.

1 Corinthians 15 v. 55: "Where, o death is your victory, where o death is your sting"

I held Anne-Marie in my arms – her head was lying in the crook of my left arm, and her legs on my lap. I looked at her and could not get over how beautiful she was. I called my sister and told her: "Look! - - -Look how beautiful she is!!" The other thing I had not expected for some reason was to feel her so warm. I said to Verena: "She's so warm! She feels warm! – Look, how beautiful she is!" And Verena just stood there with tears in her eyes.

This beautiful angelic girl in my arm, still feeling so warm, her beauty so radiant! - I was captivated, totally overcome. I can find no words to fully convey what I experienced in those precious moments... I felt *complete love* for her, enriched with joy and even some sort of elation: A silent ecstasy of love.

I just loved to look at her, to hold her, to be with her. My precious one, God bless you. My precious one, how beautiful and how lovely you are! How radiant! Pure love streamed through me and there was no tear in sight. The Holy Spirit was with us. I was so greatly blessed sitting there, holding her in my arms.

A very kind male nurse came from the ward and said to go now to a different part of the hospital, to parent rooms where Anne-Marie could get washed and dressed. I said that I wanted to do these last services for her myself and he immediately agreed. In fact the abiding memory of him, in his willingness to help and his readiness to oblige, was his consistently positive response to all my requests: "No problem."

We walked along some corridors, the male nurse, the cardiac liaison officer, Verena and I, with Anne-Marie wrapped in a blanket in my arms, along more corridors, narrower and cooler ones. I became aware of how surprisingly heavy she was but wanted to carry her all the same. Nobody was going to be allowed to come between us at this stage. If I did not give her into strangers' hands in life why should I in death? I felt it was my responsibility to ensure that no one would tamper with her dead body and to stay with her, accompanying her until her body was laid to rest.

On coming into the room, the nurse offered to take some handprints. There were different colours and papers there for this purpose. There were also scissors there to take a lock of hair. My immediate reaction to him was "No. If she was living I would play with her and make handprints but not now that she is dead," and no, I did not want to cut any hair off either.

He enquired again if I really wanted to wash her myself and if I was happy enough to stay with her while he and Verena and the liaison officer went back to the ward – all for different reasons. "Oh yes," I assured him and said, "Oh yes, I am happy to stay with her! – I love her any which way she comes." This was the truth, straight from my heart, even if it came out without much eloquence. He took a deep breath, blew it out again and said: "Phh – you're strong!"

They all left. There she was, lying on the bed on her blanket, starting to stiffen up. By the time I came to wash her, her body had become quite stiff. I put her favourite dress on her, the one she loved and had called "fancy" dress. I also put a nappy on her even though with all the fasting and vomiting there was probably no need for this.

We had to move again. This time the cardiac liaison officer came with a lovely pram for Anne-Marie. She looked so very peacefully asleep in it in her dress and blanket. I wheeled her along the corridors and my sister and I were given a side-ward back on the same heart ward we had been in from the beginning. No more word of the mortuary. We were urged to eat something as we had not eaten anything all day but thankfully Ash Wednesday came to our aid, permitting our fasting in their eyes.

There were two camp beds in our side-ward, one along each side of it, with Anne-Marie's pushchair fitting in between them at their head ends. There was also a chair next to the pram on which I had positioned her icon. The radiator was turned off and the window opened in order to keep the room cool. There was also an adjoining bathroom with toilet and shower facilities.

The side-ward was a blessing to us. I felt very thankful that the three of us were allowed to be together there. I wanted to make sure, that there would be at least one of us with her remains at all times. I saw this as an important last service that I wanted to persevere with. I felt my role was to ensure that in death as in life, Anne-Marie would not lack any love and protection I could give her - and my lovely sister was in total unity with me.

To Verena it brought back memories of the loss of her own little daughter who had died during birth (full term) many years previously. It brought back memories of a student doctor asking if the newly born was to be put in a fridge or a freezer; memories of her baby being carried off in brown paper wrapping, without having been shown to her ... Memories of fighting to retrieve Nora's remains and to be allowed to bury her... of a tiny white coffin... and of her intense pain and grief; of weeks of tearfulness and sorrow too deep to share.

Mozart's flute concertos, the only music she could bare to listen to at that time, had then become so linked with her suffering that for a while later it became impossible to listen to them. Now it was as if she was allowed to experience a healing of the wounds which the circumstances around Nora's brief coming and going had inflicted upon her. It was good for her to see and have part in ensuring that nothing untoward would happen with Anne-Marie.

The peace and love and the tranquil blessing which was upon all of us ministered to Verena. We looked at Anne-Marie again and again as she lay there as if sleeping. We both saw that especially towards the right side of her mouth and face there was a hint of a smile. Her perfect beauty was graced by the hint of a little smile. She lay there, so lovely. It was strange to see that she really was not breathing anymore. Both Verena and I found that while knowing that it was not so, once or twice it still looked to us as though she was breathing.

I wanted to lift Anne-Marie out again to hold her. I sat on my bed with her wrapped in her blanket, continually looking at her and her beauty and being so thankful to have her in my arms... and thankful also to have Verena there to share this special time.

Anne-Marie's hands were starting to loosen out again and bit by bit the stiffness left her all over. I noticed her lips toward the inside of her mouth looking very dry and slightly darker red and I remembered that I had promised her a drink "later-on." There was a pain in my heart when I realised that I had promised her a drink which I could never give her. It was hard to take in.

I put her back into the pram/pushchair. It was good to have her right next to my bed. Verena and I talked for quite a while but eventually tiredness settled on us and we gave way to drowsiness.

I was lying on my back with my right arm up above my head on the pillow and started to drift away when all of a sudden Anne-Marie's spirit came upon me with power and for a moment I had something of an identity crisis. For that moment my body felt as though it was Anne-Marie's – her little body. I had my eyes still closed and felt that I was in her small body. I had her little arm lying back and upward on my pillow and I had her little trunk and legs. Before I could follow with my mind what was happening, my own spirit had shaken off her identity and re-established itself. I was once again who I had been before. I dozed off to sleep after this experience. It was a deep and restful sleep.

1 Corinthians 15, v.42- 44: "The body that is sown is perishable, it is raised imperishable; it is sown in dishonour, it is raised in glory; it is sown in weakness, it is raised in power; it is sown a natural body, it is raised a spiritual body."

Our way home

On Thursday morning we wanted to go home as early as possible to bring Anne-Marie's remains to her family looking beautiful and like herself and to give everybody a chance to cuddle and to hold her. The next flight was not until around four in the afternoon. This seemed a long time to wait but our liaison officer urged us to settle for this flight explaining that it would probably take until then anyhow to get all the necessary papers together.

I phoned home and told Pat. He wanted to know which cemetery to contact, to try to get a plot for Anne-Marie. It was a phone-intensive day. Things changed rapidly at both ends, nearly every 15 minutes. Thankfully Verena did not mind staying with Anne-Marie while all the phone calls were going forward and backward in the corridor.

After a good friend's death I had made a number of enquiries regarding funeral practices such as make-up applied to the deceased and details of "embalming". While not all undertakers carried out exactly the same procedures, it had emerged with clarity that "embalming" was highly unnatural and not something I could subscribe to.[12] I did not wish anyone to perform this or anything like it on Anne-Marie's remains or anyone to tamper with her body in any way whatsoever.

Our liaison officer was trying her best to please us. She made many phone calls to airlines, the airport authorities and undertakers. The airport authorities would not allow the transport of a deceased person by airplane unless there was a funeral institute employed at both ends of the journey. The body of the deceased had to be embalmed and would then be carried in the coffin in the belly of the plane. Reportedly the ferry situation was the same.

Ruth 1 v. 8: "May the Lord show kindness to you as you have shown to your dead..."

The liaison officer maintained that Anne-Marie *had* to be embalmed, as this was the only way we could take her back home again. I gave in saying: "If she *has* to be embalmed, I want to be present during the procedures." Thankfully, of the many funeral directors whom she immediately went to ring there was *not one* who would have allowed me to be present during embalming. This spoke volumes to me.

I urged the liaison officer to check again with her colleague, who had assured me only yesterday that there *was* a way of getting home without embalming and was she *really* sure about the ferries? Our friendly helper showed momentary signs of weariness but went on to make more enquiries, more phone calls.

Pat had details about different cemeteries and available time slots for burial in and around Belfast. But talking it over with him, we decided that if there was no way of getting her home without embalming she should be buried in England. Now we were planning for him to drive over to Birmingham with the children. He was to find out ferry times and prices.

When the liaison officer came back, we were both bursting with news. She announced that it *was* after all possible to take Anne-Marie home *without* having her embalmed - by going by boat from Stranraer to Belfast. What a change in outlook! More phone calls. How would we get to Scotland?

The coroner decided he did *not* need to be involved for obtaining Anne-Marie's death certificate. So our helpful liaison officer and Verena were able to set off for the relevant offices in Birmingham city centre to sort out the paperwork while, with the help of the nurses, I was to rent a car to avoid travelling by public transport with a dead child in my arms. Even after countless calls we remained unsuccessful. It being the year 2000, cash deposits were a thing of the past and neither Verena nor I owned the credit card required by the car hire firms.

Dr. Simon, who had carried out Anne-Marie's admission procedures three days earlier and had enjoyed her personality and style, spotted me as I finished another phone-call. Coming over and shaking my hand, he said that he had only just heard or else he would have been over earlier. He was very sorry to hear. I invited him to come into the little sideward if he wanted, and he did.

He came in and stood there, the door behind him closing on the business of the ward, of the world. He had entered into stillness and blessing. Sunlight shining through the tilted window; he allowed the silence to speak to him, and the blessing to rest upon him. He stood and looked at Anne-Marie lying there as if asleep in her pushchair. All at once he turned around to me and said, *"I'm a Christian, too."* -

It was exhilarating to be instantly united in Christ. What a witness to the presence of the Holy Spirit filling the room! His statement, simple and profound, filled me with immense joy. It was the joy of unity in the presence of Christ, here by His Spirit.

My sister returned with all the necessary documents. The nurses were still trying one or two more car-hire firms and I thought I should check my money, in case even *one* firm might accept my idea of £100 deposit. I had not known how long we would stay and brought with me a bundle of notes which, against the very good advice of my lovely husband, I had put into my coat pocket. Now I could not find my coat. When retracing my steps I recalled that I had last had it with me outside the operating theatres around the time of Anne-Marie's death.

I went to look for my coat and found it where I had left it. I put my hand in the pockets to check for the money but there was no money. Papa's hard earned £200 had gone, disappeared in one foul sweep. 'Bless the taker' I thought. They must have needed it so much more than we. Thankfully at least they had not also needed a coat! And thankfully, too, we had not been able to book a car.

My Northern Irish cash-point card would not have worked in England, so in effect I was penniless but I refused to let this annoy me. The Lord would provide a way of getting home even without any money. All I needed was faith. I went back to Verena, coat in hand. She had not much cash either. Her chequebook and card were German and the banks were closed by now.

The ward staff were concerned that we had still not managed to settle our transport arrangements. They were beginning to wonder if in fact we were going to go at all that day.

Pat's two brothers in London both immediately dropped everything to come to our aid when they heard of our situation. James set about doing necessary repairs to his car and booked the ferry double-checking about the embalming requirements, while Brendan made his way across London to join up with James so that they could share the long drive to Scotland.

As dusk fell, Verena and I were talking together, waiting by our window for Anne-Marie's uncles to arrive from London. They were coming in James' old silver-coloured Audi coupe, which he had bought as a used car over 10 years previously and beautifully maintained all those years...It was around 8 p.m. and dark when they pulled up at the hospital.

A student nurse accompanied us down to help us with our luggage and precious load. She was moved by everything and was talking to us through watery eyes. Going down in the lift she told us the meaning of her husband's foreign sounding name. – He was named after Jesus… Somehow people felt moved to talk to us about faith with childlike openness and trust …Another blessing.

James and Brendan greeted us and arranged our luggage in the roomy boot. The suitcase was placed horizontally on top of various bags so that we could then lay Anne-Marie's body out on top of it on a blanket. The student nurse had urged us to keep a hospital blanket after I had told her to keep our folding buggy for the ward, as Anne-Marie would not need it any more. She had looked at me in amazement.

I am sure James must have bought the car for this solemn occasion all those years ago. It had been made for this journey. Everything was tangibly perfectly arranged: the two brothers sitting in the front, the two sisters sitting in the back, and Anne-Marie lying under the gently sloped window in her favourite dress with ample space around her under the stars of a clear night. No coffin, no embalming, no undertakers and no lid over her little face. What grace, what gratitude I felt - and *yes*, the Lord *had* provided a way of returning home even without a penny in my pocket.

After the journey from London the car was cosy and warm, quite unlike the early March evening temperatures outside. James, like me, likes warmth. So to keep the car cool was asking another real sacrifice. Brendan and James immediately switched off the heating in the car and even when I fancied that I had noticed their noses turning blue about half way there both of them insisted they were absolutely fine. It was not until a few months later that Brendan admitted that his feet had got so cold he could hardly feel them.

The old car performed with a touch of class. A smooth confidence-instilling ride in the spacious velvet-lined deep green seats gave it the feel of a limousine. We arrived at the harbour in Stranraer so much earlier than anticipated, that it was possible to change the booking to an earlier ferry run by a different company.

They kindly suggested for us to have the small back lounge on the top deck to ourselves. They would put a "private" notice on the door, so that we could take Anne-Marie's remains with us out of the car for the crossing. This was good news as I had already thought about hiding in the car to avoid leaving her unattended.

Approaching the ferry a little before two o'clock at night we had to pass a lit up little hut with a man sitting in it. He wanted to check the tickets, and to see Anne-Marie's death - *and embalming* certificates. I was jilted out of my blissful contentment that everything was working out so well. James asked me if I had them and I handed him what I had - a double copy of the death certificate, and a certificate stating that Anne-Marie had not suffered from infectious disease. He gave them to the man, who looked at them fleetingly, gave them back and ushered us on. "Phew!" A sigh of relief was in order.

We drove straight on, into the belly of the boat which was empty but for a few lorries. I carried Anne-Marie like a sleeping child in my arms, up the steep and narrow steps from the lower deck. Our little back lounge was lovely and cosy and *warm*. It was nice to feel the warmth after five or more hours in the cold, but of course it was not ideal for our purpose.

I found a door which opened to the outside deck and - wrapped in her blanket - I laid Anne-Marie on a solid yellow bench there. Brendan carried one of the lounge easy chairs out so that I could sit by Anne-Marie's side. At the beginning the others kept me company and then they took it in turns to come out to see if everything was all right, which it was. So eventually Anne-Marie and I travelled together by ourselves.

Matthew 8 v.27: "The men were amazed and asked, "What kind of man is this? Even the winds and the waves obey him!""

It was a clear night sky and a strikingly calm sea. It was a perfect night for homecoming, for travelling under the stars of the vast expanse of the universe, mirrored in the deep black sea, on an intimate and last journey together. Nature was looking on, peacefully surrounding us, respectfully accompanying, supporting her child's last journey - knowing about our little Anne-Marie's homecoming. A breeze of wind moved a tuft of hair on her forehead. How lovely she was.

Yes, Anne-Marie's body had got cold by now; but it looked and felt so relaxed, so at peace. I was looking at her little face, her lovely features, her lips… and a pang of regret crept up in my mind and heart. Her dry lips reminded me of my empty and forever unfulfillable promise of getting her a drink. I so much wanted to make this up to her! I saw a drop of water on the yellow bench and, lifting it onto my finger, I gently moistened her lips while speaking with her and appeasing my own soul saying, "There, take this little drop of water to moisten your lips". Strangely my pain subsided from that moment. Somehow I had fulfilled my promise and I felt she accepted it, even now.

With the outside lights switched off for the journey, I could see the others chatting inside the warm lit-up lounge. It was like two different worlds. I arranged myself in my lounge chair and coat, so as not to get too cold. I had my hood tied up tightly and my knees drawn up under the zipped up coat. Sitting on the sleeves I kept my arms inside to stay warm. I quietly sang and hummed my favourite praise songs to Anne-Marie to accompany her on her passage and also to keep me awake.

In my progressively sleepy state I thought I had heard myself sing not quite the correct words of one of these songs. Indeed, I had changed them without even being aware of it, singing: "*She sent me to give the good news to the poor…*" instead of "***He sent me to give the good news to the poor…***" I had to smile to myself. *She*, Anne-Marie, now joined with *Him*, Our Lord, would indeed send me to give the good news to the poor… Some steps approached from behind and a man walked by. I will never know what - if anything - he thought, seeing us there.

It was getting light as we were approaching Belfast harbour. It was a beautiful morning - a clear soft blue sky with just a hint of a few lines of white clouds. It was Friday, 10 March 2000. I carried my precious pale darling down the steep and narrow steps and laid her out arranging the blanket so that she would not easily be seen by anyone behind the car.

We pulled up in front of our house at around seven in the morning. Spring was in the air. We were getting out of the car just as our friend Suzanne came cycling round the corner with a little card in her hand. She had intended to push this through our door, not to disturb us. Seeing us arrive caught her completely unawares. I showed her Anne-Marie's beautiful and peaceful remains. She looked as if she were sleeping. Suzanne was overcome by tears.

Somehow I was at such a different place from most people. I did not even really understand why they should cry. To me something wondrous and beautiful had happened, something that was peaceful and right as God's peace had not left us at any stage...

Pat and the children had only just got up. They welcomed us home in their pyjamas. The children wanted to see Anne-Marie. I sat them down on the stairs and everyone got to hold and to cuddle her. Papa held her, too. I think I saw a little tear in Papa's eye, but the children were not crying although they were looking serious and sombre. It was good to hold her; it was good to see that it was really her, our little darling.

Five years later (and beyond) Raphael still remembered that at the time he was surprised that he did not feel sad, as he had thought that he should have. He recalled that everything felt so natural and right that sadness just did not enter in.

How different it would have been to arrive with her in a box, accompanied by strangers dressed in black. No, nothing was wrong. Everything flowed, everything happened just as it should have. No strangers had taken over, nobody had taken her away from us and tampered with her body and nobody had done anything that was our privilege to do. The family was intact and united around Anne-Marie's remains.

Papa had bought a white coffin from a friend in the country, who is a farmer and undertaker and it was waiting for her to be bedded in it. I had passed on Anne-Marie's height measurements from Birmingham so the coffin was just the right size. It looked pretty, but unnatural. There was a white polyester lace trimming around the top. On the outside, it was covered with white jacquard cloth while the inside was lined with white plastic.

The thought of Anne-Marie's remains being kept from uniting themselves with the earth because of plastic around them did not appeal to me. I enquired with everyone in the family if they would mind if I removed the lining of the coffin. Nobody objected and so I ripped out all the inside of the coffin, getting – I must admit – some satisfaction from the very act of doing this. It felt so right, so cleansing, to rip away all the alienation from the life and death cycle and to facilitate instead its long established ordained workings. What was left was a coffin looking white from the outside with plywood showing on the inside. And yes, that was fine. We lovingly wrapped Anne-Marie's body in a crisp-white cotton bath towel and gently bedded her inside.

In order to keep her remains cool we positioned the little coffin onto the tiled floor of the lower kitchen, which was the coolest place in the house. Solemn and united, at peace and at one with each other, we gathered in serenity around the remains of our beautiful and peaceful looking youngest member of our family and took some photographs. Her race had been run. She had reached the finish line before any of us. She had completed her tasks on earth and entered into the heavenly realms at the tender age of two years and seven months, leaving a profound impact on the lives of many people.

Our little princess, our chuckling, our darling "character" - the funniest one of us all, as Pascal described her - had come to the end of suffering. She had reached an age, which had allowed her to be abundantly involved in life. She had completely immersed herself in it and had without any reservation taken part in everything that had been on offer within our family setting.

She had been able to name everything, including even the difficult-to-pronounce (then in vogue) Pokemon characters. She had known the trees, the sun, the clouds, the rain, the heat and the cold. She knew about people and animals, about joy and mischief, about suffering and perseverance, about fear and love, about God.

She had entered life fully, living each moment with the intensity of her spiritual intelligence.

She had also died at an age where her spirit had not been broken. She did not have to learn that this big and colourful world does not offer everyone the same opportunities, that things are not always as good and as exciting as they seem, and that she would have been painfully limited when competing with her peers. Was this not the girl who, when her big brothers and sister had a race up the stairs at bedtime, would not let breathlessness beat her and instead used all her strength and willpower to hasten up the stairs behind them as fast as she could?

Anne-Marie had come home and her family was around her now. A busy day was ahead of us and having had no sleep on the way over, I felt I could lie down now and take a rest.

The Wake

When I got up again I heard that I had missed Fr. Colm's first visit, but other visitors were arriving. Thankful to have had a shower the previous morning, I went downstairs to be there with the visitors. I felt so blessed, so excited, and so thankful about all of Anne-Marie's life, about everything to do with her homecoming; I had felt God's gentle presence, his peace, love and joy so close, so real that I did not want anyone to misunderstand what had happened. There was a sense of celebration and elation with me which some of the visitors found bewildering.

We still had the little coffin on the floor in the back kitchen. Papa thought it was not a bad idea, as it required people to get on their knees if they wanted to be close to her. He always had a wonderful way of seeing things. This worked fine until one of our visitors had difficulties kneeling down. I lifted the coffin up a little, apologetically conceding that maybe we should put it elsewhere. Our visitor instantly took over and organised the kitchen table to become the place for the coffin. This was difficult to reverse without stepping on her toes. I became inwardly irritable. Thankfully Pat managed to diffuse the situation but the incident left me feeling disappointed that it was so easy for me to loose my peace.

One way or another, the little coffin had unceremoniously arrived on the kitchen table and was perched at the end of it, at right angles to it. Having not yet regained my peace, I felt quite unable to change things for the better so this was where it stayed for the time being.

The arrival of Sinead and Cathleen from the Siloam Community *instantly* brought back the presence of the Holy Spirit, yes, the *joy* of His presence. I was bubbling over talking of Anne-Marie, of all that had happened, of the highlights of her life, of her heavenly smile and even joyful giggle at the end, of the wonderful journey back,… from before her conception story to the angel singing on the telephone… Everything wanted to get told again, just to let them know the wonder of her life, the wonder of the finger of God in her life - and in all our lives. They were lively listeners and from their arrival onwards the presence and the joy of the Holy Spirit established itself in the house and remained with us.

Cathleen and Sinead were the right people to sit vigil with Anne-Marie's remains. I slipped out to buy some flowers for her. The local shops did not have any pink roses. The only fresh pink flowers they had were pink white-edged tulips. Back home I placed the tulips along the inside edges of the coffin so that she was framed by them, looking beautiful.

As more people came, bringing their cards and flowers, we rearranged the table, putting a white tablecloth on and placing the coffin long-ways on the top, with flowers at the head-end and cards along both sides. This was her final resting position in our house.

Many more people came. Some had come from a distance, from Co. Tyrone and some even from Dublin. Two untiring friends - both called Eileen - were working around the clock to provide teas and coffees, biscuits and sandwiches.

Fr. Colm McBride called again to discuss the details for the next morning. He advised us that we could choose the Old Testament reading, the Psalm and the New Testament reading for Anne-Marie's Mass, which had been arranged for nine a.m. the following morning, while he would like to choose the Gospel reading. We were also to organise the readers. He was happy with our choice of songs which Sharon had put together on song-sheets.

It was wonderful to be surrounded by so many people of genuine faith. Indeed there were reports that some experienced a renewal of their dormant faith while others left simply amazed. Fergus expanded on my own awareness of the earlier part of Anne-Marie's story: When I had just retold the part of how Pat, at Anne-Marie's birth, had said "You were right all along," Fergus enquired if Pat had not also suffered from being unable to speak prior to this time! (- giving us all a good laugh.) He was relating it to John the Baptist's father Zechariah, who through lack of faith, had had to endure a period of dumbness… (*Luke, chapter 1*)

By around 9:30pm the last callers had left and it was now time to decide which readings to choose. The Old Testament reading, Isaiah 40, was easy to pick, as Anne-Marie had come 'through' St. John the Baptist's icon and in his spirit of preparing the way, the spirit of The Forerunner as he is called in the Orthodox Church.

For the reading of the Psalm we tried to locate the Psalm sung to me over the telephone, which had dispelled all darkness and which had made the praise of the Lord the most important and blessed thing to do especially since then. We decided that the Psalm was Psalm 103 (Western numbering)...and have kept to this, even though I now think it might have been Psalm 104.

But how could we find the right reading from the New Testament? Of course, there is no shortage of important, meaningful and beautiful passages, but which one was the right one for Anne-Marie?

Once the children were asleep I was sitting on the settee with my bible on my knees, leafing through and looking fairly aimlessly at various different passages of the New Testament in the hope that one might, so to speak, jump out at me but none did. Papa was in the kitchen studying the suggested readings which Fr. Colm had left. Neither of us could decide on a reading that was specifically for Anne-Marie and I could sense a touch of irritation rising within our Papa, which is most atypical for him.

Revelation 3 v. 21: "To him who overcomes I will give the right to sit with me on my throne..."

As we were wrestling with finding the right New Testament reading, the doorbell rang. At this time of the night? A most apologetic Norma was standing in our unlit porch with her bible under her arm. She said she had been in two minds whether or not to come at this late hour, hm-ing and ha-ing about it at home, until her husband pointed out that it would be better to go now rather than to spend more time wondering about it and then still to go. She had driven up from the other side of Belfast to tell me a most wonderful story:

The Siloam Community heard about Anne-Marie's death when it was announced at the beginning of their Thursday night meeting. Norma said she had been very affected by the news and that her tears were flowing, even while singing praises to God with the community. She said she could not help crying for the emptiness of my arms.

I butted in and said, "Norma, your prayers were answered, because I did not have to give Anne-Marie out of my arms to anyone else at all," and told her something of Anne-Marie's homecoming but her story was not finished. During the (extensive) praise she received a picture, a vision, to comfort her. She saw the white Hall of Glory with Our Lord sitting there on His Throne with Anne-Marie in the crook of his arm! The two of them there together, as happy…

I was overwhelmed, excited, thankful - awestruck. This was wonderful. Of course that was where she was! Yes, I had no doubt that the vision had depicted the spiritual reality and truth about Anne-Marie's whereabouts. But what Grace to be shown it!

And she had more news. She told me that she felt the Lord had given her a reading specifically for Anne-Marie, even in the week leading up to her death. She opened her bible in the New Testament at Philippians chapter 1 and explained that while she had felt directed to the whole passage of verses 3-11 and that the sentence: *"He, who began a good work in you will carry it on to completion until the day of Christ Jesus"* had particularly stood out to her for Anne-Marie.

Of course Norma was not aware that she had called at a time when we had been searching for a New Testament reading for Anne-Marie. Quite unbeknown to her she had become a messenger of the Lord. He Himself had provided the right reading through her. I shared my excitement with her. How perfect: The Lord's timing and provision. Everything was coming together.

Just before heading up to bed myself, Sharon, called "Mummy 2" (Or Mummy, too?) by Anne Marie, came to bid her last farewell. She brought a single pink rose with a very short bit of stem. She gave it to me and I slipped it into Anne-Marie's hands. This was its perfect place. Anne-Marie had even received her pink rose. We bedded down for a short night's sleep as no one had felt the necessity to sit up with Anne-Marie this night. She was at home.

Ecclesiastes 6 v.5: "A man may have 100 children and live many years; yet no matter how long he lives, if he cannot enjoy his prosperity and does not receive proper burial, I say that a stillborn child is better off than he."

The Day of the Funeral

Looking in my wardrobe I decided to wear the dress a lady had given me at the "Baptism by fire"-course. This was the dress I looked upon as my wedding dress to the Lord. It had light green patterns, flowers. It was immediately obvious that this should be worn with the pastel green thank-you-for-Glassie fleece. I was dressed but for my feet.

The morning turned out a little hectic with getting the children ready while the first people arrived to join in with the prayers at the house. Our Papa led the prayers in the kitchen before closing the coffin. His undertaker-friend was on stand-by. Quite a crowd had gathered in the kitchen and the hall, some of them having travelled for hours to be with us.

One of Pat's cousins arrived after the coffin was already closed but still on the kitchen table, so we opened it up again for her to have one last look at our lovely little darling with her chubby cheeks, her china-doll appearance, surrounded by pink and white tulips and holding her little rose in her hands. It was a moving sight and the cousin's eyes filled with tears.

We closed the lid again and fastened the photograph of the statue of Saint Joseph holding the Christ child on top of the coffin.

Pat folded away the backseats of our little white Citroen AX, the car of his deceased brother, and spread out a tartan-patterned woolly blanket, and yes, the coffin fitted in lengthwise.

Raphael, Pascal and Alma, by now aged eight, six and four, hopped into the back with the remains of their precious little sister. I took my place in the front passenger seat and Pat drove the whole family to church. How fitting it was, that we had a *white* car, Kevin's car, rather than a black limousine for her last journey; a white car for the white coffin, for the little girl with the white soul, not contaminated by anything.

Isaiah 35 v. 10: "Gladness and joy will overtake them, and sorrow and sighing will flee away."

"The Mass of the Angels," Anne-Marie's funeral Mass, was to start at 9 a.m. at our local St. Therese's Catholic Church. This was the same church where Anne-Marie had been christened and Fr. Mc Bride, her priest, was the celebrant. There was a great multitude of people waiting for us at the chapel and it was impossible to speak with them all. I talked to only a few and proceeded towards the church doors.

Just as we were going in, I spotted Fiona. Fiona! It had been my secret desire that our Old Testament reading from Isaiah 40 should ring out through the church in form of the aria *"|:Every valley shall be exalted:| And every high place made low,"* from Handel's Messiah and here was Fiona, our ex choir-mistress with the most beautiful resounding alto voice, standing by the entry doors to the chapel! Another divine appointment. I quickly asked her to please sing it as a communion reflection. I knew she would do it justice. I was delighted.

The whole family carried the little coffin in together. Papa and Mummy, Raphael, Pascal and Alma walked up the middle aisle carrying our Anne-Marie's remains to the front of the church. We carefully positioned the little coffin on the stand by the steps in front of the altar and took our places in the front row on the right hand side of the church as this had been left free for us. The church was well filled and many more people came in after we had entered.

To the left at the front was a little group from the Siloam Community, with David and his guitar leading their dedicated praises to God. Sharon's song-sheets had been handed out. I was charged with wanting to give praise, thanks, and glory to God, for this, His wonderful child – I was filled with His Spirit to overflowing.

The first song started:

> *"He set me free one day, He set me free.*
> *He broke the bars of the prison for me*
> *I'm glory bound my Saviour to see,*
> *Praise the Lord He set me free"*

…and again, and again, and again. The Siloam community certainly were not afraid to sing a song more than once. It was good, it was needed and it set the scene. We were here to celebrate Anne-Marie's return to the Saviour and even those who might have been unfamiliar with this little chorus were able to join in after hearing it once or twice. And so it was, that everybody seemed to join in.

Mine was the first reading, the Old Testament reading: Isaiah 40 v.3-9. I stepped up the steps to the stand, adjusted the microphone and began to read. – "A reading from the prophet Isaiah." The Holy Spirit was upon me. I read with authority.

> *A voice of one calling:*
>
> *"In the desert prepare the way for the Lord*
> *Make straight in the wilderness*
> *A highway for our God.*
> *Every valley shall be raised up,*
> *Every mountain and hill made low;*
> *The rough ground shall become level,*
> *The rugged places a plain.*
> *And the glory of the Lord will be revealed,*
> *And all mankind together will see it.*
> *For the mouth of the Lord has spoken."*
>
> *A voice says, "Cry out."*
> *And I said, "What shall I cry?"*
>
> *"All men are like grass,*
> *And all their glory is like the flowers of the field.*
> *The grass withers and the flowers fall,*
> *Because the breath of the Lord blows on them.*
> *Surely the people are grass.*
> *The grass withers and the flowers fall,*
> *But the word of our God stands for ever."*
>
> . . .

"…This *is* the word of the Lord".

His word stood there from time immemorial, majestically, full of life and strength, full of radiance and truth and full of the presence of the Lord, resounding through the chapel, hovering over the congregation who according to some people's comments later on were taken completely unawares. Like me, they had not expected to meet with the breath of the Lord.

Brian read Psalm 103:

Praise the Lord, O my soul;

> *All my inmost being, praise his holy name.*
> *Praise the Lord, O my soul,*
> *And forget not all his benefits –*
> *Who forgives all your sins*
> *And heals all your diseases,*
> *Who redeems your life from the pit*
> *And crowns you with love and compassion,*
> *Who satisfies your desires with good things*
> *So that your youth is renewed like the eagle's.*

Praise the Lord, O my soul

> *The Lord works righteousness and justice*
> *For all the oppressed.*
> *He made known his ways to Moses,*
> *His deeds to the people of Israel:*
> *The Lord is compassionate and gracious,*
> *Slow to anger, abounding in love.*
> *He will not always accuse,*
> *Nor will he harbour his anger forever;*
> *He does not treat us as our sins deserve*
> *Or repay us according to our iniquities.*

Praise the Lord, O my soul

> *For as high as the heavens are above the earth,*
> *So great is his love for those who fear him;*
> *As far as the East is from the West,*
> *So far has he removed our transgressions from us.*
> *As a father has compassion on his children,*

So the Lord has compassion on those who fear him;

Praise the Lord O my soul

> *For he knows how we are formed,*
> *He remembers that we are dust.*
> *As for man, his days are like grass,*
> *He flourishes like a flower of the field;*
> *The wind blows over it and it is gone,*
> *And its place remembers it no more.*
> *But from everlasting to everlasting*
> *The Lord's love is with those who fear him'*
> *And his righteousness with their children's children –*
> *With those who keep his covenant*
> *And remember to obey his precepts.*

Praise the Lord, O my soul

> *The Lord has established his throne in heaven,*
> *And his kingdom rules over all.*
> *Praise the Lord, you his angels,*
> *You mighty ones who do his bidding,*
> *Who obey his word,*
> *Praise the Lord all his heavenly hosts,*
> *You his servants who do his will.*
> *Praise the Lord all his works*
> *Everywhere in his dominion.*
> *Praise the Lord, O my soul*

Praise the Lord, O my soul

I am not sure how the psalm arrived with everyone else but I was still so overwhelmed by the previous reading that it nearly passed me by. It was not until later that the similarity of the theme struck me, that they both compare our life on earth to that of a flower of the field – certainly a beautiful little flower in Anne-Marie's case. How befitting that the very church we were in was dedicated to "The Little Flower" St. Therese of Lisieux, a saint who did not make it into ripe old age, either.

Norma read Anne-Marie's reading:

Philippians 1:3-11

> *I thank my God every time I remember you. In all my prayers for all of you, I always pray with joy because of your partnership in the gospel from the first day until now, being confident of this, that <u>He who began a good work in you will carry it on to completion until the day of Christ Jesus.</u>*
>
> *It is right for me to feel this way about all of you, since I have you in my heart; for whether I am in chains or defending and confirming the gospel, all of you share in God's grace with me. God can testify how I long for all of you with the affection of Christ Jesus.*
>
> *<u>And this is my prayer: That your love may abound more and more in knowledge and depth of insight, so that you may be able to discern what is best and may be pure and blameless until the day of Christ, filled with the fruit of righteousness that comes through Jesus Christ - to the glory and praise of God.</u>*

This was Anne-Marie, talking to each and every one, even to you who are reading this. … And here you have the advantage. You can read over it again and again. In the church everything happened so quickly - already it was Fr. McBride's turn to read the Gospel. He had chosen a passage from St. Matthew's Gospel: Mat.11 v.25-30 (he read from a different translation):

> *At that time Jesus said: "I praise you, Father, Lord of heaven and earth, because you have hidden these things from the wise and learned, and revealed them to little children. Yes, Father, for this was your good pleasure.*

All things have been committed to me by my Father. No one knows the Son except the Father, and no one knows the Father except the Son and those to whom the Son chooses to reveal him.

Come to me, all you who are weary and burdened, and I will give you rest. Take my yoke upon you and learn from me, for I am gentle and humble in heart, and you will find rest for your souls. For my yoke is easy and my burden is light."

"*...and revealed them to little children.*" This phrase resounded with me. Yes, I was sure that this applied to Anne-Marie. But all of the reading was so good to hear. I did not feel weary or burdened at the time, but it was relieving to think of this gentle and humble Lord; it was peace-giving to know where rest could be found and to have Him invite us: "*Come to me.*"

Fr Mc Bride addressed the congregation with a story about himself and his brother when they were boys. One day the two of them came upon a place in the forest where there was a beautiful carpet of flowering bluebells. When they went to look at them more closely, to their great surprise they found that in among all these pretty bluebells there was *one*, just one, which looked like a bluebell in every way except for one thing: it was *white*.

He talked about how nature just occasionally changes things a little, how it brings forth something somewhat different from the norm and compared this to Anne-Marie's heart. His gentle and sensitive words, also about Anne-Marie herself, were warmly received by everyone. Anne-Marie was now our pure white bluebell, the little flower of the field which the breath of the Lord had blown upon.

The offertory procession came to the altar. Raphael and Pascal were bringing gifts of bread and wine while Alma brought something representing Anne-Marie – a "Little Miss" toy. I was surprised to hear the sound of a tin whistle. A haunting Celtic-sounding melody filled the air. It was Cathy Curran, playing a tune called "The Women of Ireland."

Fr. McBride beautifully celebrated the consecration in song. We all stood up to pray the "Our Father" - which, as an afterthought, might also have been nice sung - Again the solid unity of those present commanded an extra blessing.

Two Eucharistic ministers helped to give out Communion *under both species*. My heart's desire had been granted – how humbling and how wonderful - the full presence of Our Lord, in both body and forgiveness-bringing blood was here, available for strengthening purifying and filling us with His love, with Himself to overflowing.

Our response to him found expression in the Communion song, led by the Siloam Community:

> *My Jesus, my Saviour,*
> *Lord there is none like you,*
> *All of my days I want to praise*
> *The wonders of your mighty love;*
>
> *My comfort, my shelter,*
> *Tower of refuge and strength,*
> *Let every breath, all that I am,*
> *Never cease to worship you.*
>
> *Shout to the Lord all the earth, let us sing,*
> *Power and majesty, praise to the King,*

Mountains bow down and the seas will roar
At the sound of your name,

I sing for joy at the work of your hands
Forever I love you, forever I stand,
Nothing compares to the promise I have
In you.

There was a wonderful presence of the Lord. The sound of praise to the Lord built up to a fantastic strength and carried me towards freedom. I forgot all about everything around me and entered without restraint into singing praises and before I knew it - the song was being sung maybe the third time at this stage - I entered freedom from self. Without even realising it I found myself singing out a harmony to the main melody at the top of my voice, my heart bursting with the joy of the presence of the Holy Spirit. What a wonderful, solid tidal wave of community praise, immersing us in a foretaste of Heaven.

After Communion silence fell. Fr. McBride looked around and there was Fiona coming from the far left of the front of the church and stepped forward. Her clear, strong and beautiful alto voice filled the air. Thousands of years were bridged yet again, when Isaiah's words were proclaimed in song: (from Handel's Messiah)

Every valley shall be exalted, shall be exalted,
And every high place made low
And every high place made low

Every valley shall be exalted…

Those beautiful turns of melody, going over the same words again and again, that they will be heard and indelibly engraved in every part of our being to bring forth fruit, - faith. Faith which will continue the work of St. John, of preparing the way, of making straight in the wilderness of our hearts, of our lives, a highway for our God,

> *...shall be exalted,*
> *And every high place made low...*

...so that there is no rugged path, no stone nor pebble left in the way to hinder Our Lord's coming to turn our wasteland, our deserts into fertile ground, with springs and rivers...

All the parts of the Mass were alive, full of meaning. All the responses, all the prayers – everything was Spirit-filled. Anne-Marie's remains were blessed and surrounded by beautifully fragrant incense and before long it was time for the last hymn to be sung:

> *(S-)***He sent me to give the good news...**
> *God's Spirit is in my heart,*
> *He has called me and set me apart,*
> *This is what I have to do,*
> *What I have to do*

This being a longer hymn with quite a few verses, Fr McBride came over to us after it had started and suggested that we might want to carry out the coffin with Anne-Marie's remains while it was sung.

He sent me to give the good news to the poor,
Tell prisoners that they are prisoners no more,
Tell blind people that they can see,
And set the downtrodden free,
And go, tell everyone
The news that the Kingdom of God has come,
And go, tell everyone
The news that God's Kingdom has come.

Papa, Raphael, Pascal, Alma and I went up to the middle of the front of the church where Anne-Mare's little coffin was, lifted it off its little stand and started to carry it down the aisle: Papa at the front, Mummy at the back and the children on either side, the singing resounding all around us.

Just as the father sent me,
So I'm sending you out to be
My witnesses throughout the world,
The whole of the world.

(S-)He sent me to give the good news to the poor
Tell prisoners that they are prisoners no more…

I was engrossed in singing the song, remembering that this indeed *was* her message to me…

…Tell blind people that they can see,
And set the downtrodden free,
And go, tell everyone…

…but could not help noticing that there were lots of red looking eyes among the people of the congregation.

…The news that the Kingdom of God has come,
And go, tell everyone the news that

God's Kingdom has come!...

Just then, for a flash of an instant, Papa turned round and looked at me, and I saw his pain. His face had turned red and I saw a tear coming from his eye - our lovely Papa, - Help him, Lord!

> *Don't carry a load in your pack,*
> *You don't need two shirts on your back,*
> *A workman can earn his own keep,*
> *Can earn his own keep.*

Only now, coming down the aisle, I realised that the chapel was filled to the last seat with rows and rows of people on both sides and more standing at the back. How many people were touched by this child of God; how many wanted to be associated with her!

> *...He sent me to give the good news to the poor,*
> *Tell prisoners that they are prisoners no more,...*

We were coming to the doors of the chapel and just continued walking to our little white Citroen. The singing continued inside the chapel while we were trying to reposition the little coffin in the back of the car.

> *...Don't worry what you have to say,*
> *Don't worry because on that day,*
> *God's Spirit will speak in your heart,*
> *Will speak in your heart...*

Having not thought of any form of protocol, we were standing by the back of the car when people came out of the chapel. They did not have an opportunity to shake hands with us on their way out but once they had located us, a long queue formed of people wanting to express their sympathy.

There were relations, friends and neighbours from Belfast and Tyrone, from Dublin, Down and South Armagh. A host of different organisations were represented. "The Lamb of God Community" and "The Siloam Community" were with us, members of the Focolare-movement including Lieta (R.I.P) had travelled all the way from Dublin to be here for this 9 a.m. Mass, Corrymeela was represented as was the Columbanus community. There were members of NIMMA (Northern Irish Mixed Marriage Association) and the principle and other representatives of Hazelwood Integrated Primary School, where our children were pupils, as well as people from the North Belfast "Homestart" organisation who had helped us during Anne-Marie's lifetime and representatives of Pat's workplace.

An Anglican minister and many members of the Protestant community had been side by side with an Orthodox deacon and representatives of the Orthodox community all united in prayer and praise with Catholic Christians and a Catholic priest in our local Church.

The faith-unity of all the committed believers instilled a deep joy within me and left an impression on those with less fervent faith. Anne-Marie had made it possible, here in Belfast, Northern Ireland, in this day and age (March 2000) to have clergy and lay people of the three main Christian traditions united in prayer and praise of God without any question or holding back.

We had to speed things up. People were already arriving for the ten o'clock Saturday morning Mass and we were also tied to a time-slot at Carnmoney cemetery. We were not able to continue shaking hands but headed out towards the cemetery through the big gates which Fr. McBride had kindly opened. A large black limousine or a hearse would have been useful at this point to lead the way, and as it happened there were a few minor mix-ups of people not knowing who to follow but as far as I am aware everybody who wanted to be there found their way to the graveyard.

To get to Anne-Marie's plot one had to drive through much of the older part of the cemetery into a newer area which was separated from the main part a little by trees, shrubs and hedges. It felt nice and secluded. Fr. McBride was awaiting us. Papa had told him the location of the plot after the Mass.

The graves were identified by letters and numbers and Anne-Marie's plot was 'OK99'. I smiled an inward smile. Anne-Marie had had a liking for expressing her agreement to something by saying 'OK' and 1999 had been her best year.

It was a clear and windy day. We were carrying the coffin to the grave, the location of which I did not know, when Pat asked pleadingly if I would mind if these people here carried the coffin for just the short stretch of the way to the grave – they would give it back to us at the graveside to lower down. I was not fully aware what was happening and was guided by the pleading look on Pat's face for my decision.

So, before I knew it, two gravediggers were carrying Anne-Marie's remains the few yards up to the graveside. I felt a sinking feeling. Why had I fought so hard to not give her into strangers' hands up to this point only to give her away yards before her final place of rest? Two or three yards and we were by her side again ready to attend to her.

We were given the broad bands to hold, which had been fed through the handles and underneath the coffin. As this was the first coffin to go into our family grave, it was really very deep. We carefully lowered the little white coffin. The photograph of Saint Joseph, holding the Christ-child was looking up towards us. Looking down onto the little coffin in the grave, the photograph was strangely reassuring. She was somehow not alone.

Standing at the head end of the grave with the children, I commented to them about being careful not to overbalance or else we would end up on top of her! Alma and Pascal, chilled by the cool winds, ended up wrapped in my coat with me while Fr McBride conducted a prayer service at the graveside. We were all invited to put a little shovel full of sand into the grave and wooden boards were positioned across the top of the open grave soon after. One or two little bunches of flowers came to lie on them even though we had asked for donations to Clark Clinic in lieu of flowers.

A great many people had come to the graveside and we had a houseful of people afterwards. People were struck by the Mass and even now, over seven years later, comments are still being made that this Mass was an outstanding experience... Raphael had called it the most wonderful Mass he had ever been to on the day.

Lieta, our old friend and 'Capozona' for Ireland of the Focolare movement was visibly receptive to all the unusual wondrous and wonderful details of Anne-Marie's life, encouraging me also to write this book. Another reason for the timing of Anne-Marie's death struck me when speaking to her. I had always felt that Anne-Marie had been behind my project of the "Come and See" charity shop[17]. It suddenly seemed obvious that she had also left to be a help for the project coming to fruition, this time from above, rather than being a hindrance by being a sickly child needing plenty of attention. It seemed she had gone at this time - out of love.

Isaiah 61 v 1-3: "He has sent me... to comfort all who mourn, and provide for those who grieve in Zion—to bestow on them a crown of beauty instead of ashes, the oil of gladness instead of mourning, and a garment of praise instead of a spirit of despair. They will be called oaks of righteousness, a planting of the Lord for the display of his splendour."

Life after Death

Verena's family was grief-stricken and unable to make sense of this 'early' death of their cousin and niece. Returning to Germany, she had the difficult task of bringing something of the presence of the Spirit with her to comfort her loved ones at home.

This was also my task here at home and among my relations, friends and acquaintances in various locations, and in a way it is even now. Thankfully, every time I have the opportunity to share events of Anne-Marie's life, there seems to be an ever-replenishing supply of energy bubbling forth from within me. Anne-Marie's story is forever new and exciting – energy giving, life-giving – for me.

My parents were filled with awe and wonder when hearing about all the things that had taken place and they in turn were able to pass 'the good news' of Anne-Marie sitting in the crook of Jesus' arms on to the wider family circle in Germany.

Monday came. The children went to school, Pat went to work and I was left in the house by myself wondering how this would go. I felt I had a choice, an almost daunting choice of what I should do. I hesitated for a while and then decided to not forget what I had learned: To face any potentially difficult situations with praise of God.

Nehemiah 8 v. 10: "Do not grieve for the joy of the Lord is your strength."

I went upstairs to the bathroom to deal with the huge backlog of washing while singing praises to God. I started to hang up the wet washing singing praises while at the same time carefully observing myself as to how I was feeling but it was fine. It was eminently possible to do it in this way. There was no need to be afraid.

Towards the end of the afternoon a neighbour man came carrying Alma, our four-year-old, on his arm. She had fallen off Pascal's bike and was crying but had no cuts or bruises. She spent the rest of the day on the settee and was carried up to bed later. Early next morning when she could not walk to the toilet I realised that her cycling injury was probably more serious than I had thought.

At the children's hospital we were sent for an x-ray just to be sure. It was strange to be in the position of holding my daughter for the purpose of her having an x-ray after doing the same for Anne-Marie only a week ago – it felt a little like a 'take-two'. Alma's shinbone had been broken right through and her leg had to be put in plaster. We were told that she would have to be admitted for observation.

We were allocated a bed at the far end of a Florence Nightingale-type ward. It felt unreal. We were to spend the day and night in the children's hospital - just in case I had been in danger of forgetting what that was like. It seemed significant that this should be happening at precisely one week after Anne-Marie's last day and night in hospital

As part of the routine admission procedures Alma was checked out from top to bottom. The admission doctor informed us that Alma had a slight heart murmur and that he would refer her to the cardiologists. I thought I was hearing things. The whole thing took on a dream-like quality. He assured us that this was quite common and probably quite harmless, but he just wanted it checked out now that she was here anyhow...

There was the electrocardiogram, the echo-scan and of course here came the arm cuff and blood pressure machine... Seeing it approach I noticed dread rising within me. Yet, as the nurse was taking Alma's blood pressure my inward knots were loosened bit by bit. It was not a torture-machine after all but a harmless and painless gadget for collecting important medical information...

By the time the nurse was pushing the machine away again a healing had taken place within me. I was able to relate normally to the diagnostic medical gadgets and procedures. All their connotations as heralds of suffering and death had in a most peaceable way been peeled off and removed. Maybe *this* was the reason for all these things happening – maybe without this experience I would have been left with a fear of this type of medical machinery?

Dr. Craig came to visit us during his lunch hour. He enquired about Alma but we also spent a long time in conversation about things to do with Anne-Marie. He was interested in every aspect of what had happened, both from the human/compassionate and the professional viewpoints and was alive to all the details. Some of his comments had a ring of timeless truth to them, such as the insight that after the death of someone close one feels that things should not just return to run as normal. He had a finely tuned understanding of the person of Anne-Marie and said many wise and helpful things when pondering her specific life and impact on others. One of these, which stood out to me as something akin to a prophecy contained the thought that *we would probably find that her story would continue to unfold through time.*

(*Compare:* "He, who began a good work in you, will carry it on to completion")

Alma's nurse was very sympathetic when she heard about Anne-Marie and told us about her own brother. How remarkable to think that her own brother's anniversary was also on 8 March! Of all the nurses in the hospital, the Lord had arranged for us to be seen by this one...

Alma was allowed home the following day with her leg in plaster. She greatly enjoyed being my little sofa-princess and the centre of attention. For me, too, it was lovely to have her at home to pamper and be close to and while other people might have wondered about yet another disaster coming our way, to us it was really a blessed time of nest-warmth and closeness.

During the days and weeks which followed Anne-Marie's death our little family was drawing closer together. The children were noticeably more open toward one another and also to us, their parents. We spent a lot of time talking about Anne-Marie and how now that she was with God, because God is everywhere, she could be everywhere, too. How many other children had such a special little sister who could be with each one of them anywhere and at any time?

Everybody remembered different things about her and it always felt as though she was not too far away. At meal times we might have remembered how she had put her not-quite-empty bowl of spaghetti on her head upside-down and when driving past a McDonald's somebody would call out "McDonald's, McDonald's" just the way she would have done; or coming in from outside someone remembered how she used to pull off her little hat and drop it onto the floor saying 'back home!' whenever she came in.

Some things that came to light were new even to me! Apparently she had loved playing "shop," pretending that one corner in the hall downstairs was a shop where she used to go and ask for chewing-gum (banned in our house) whenever I was not looking and then, returning to her brothers and sister, she would hand out pretend chewing-gum packets to everyone. Pascal said that she was the funniest of all of us and he was right. He was also the one who had said to his auntie Verena that she need not worry because Anne-Marie was now a Saint in Heaven.

We received a steady flow of Mass cards, sympathy cards and letters of condolence from people near and far, often testifying how Anne-Marie had touched their lives. There were also unusual letters and occurrences: Sharon's daughter Danielle (11) made a little poem about Anne-Marie and her beloved St. "Jophes". She had also had a dream in which she saw Anne-Marie running in a summer meadow and playing together with Jesus and gave me a little biro drawing of this scene.

Another friend of ours, who had met Anne-Marie only a few times, was very upset when he heard of her death. Much like Norma he received a vision capturing Anne-Marie's happiness in Jesus' company in the middle of being grief stricken. He wrote:

"...and while I was crying I had a sudden glimpse of Jesus holding Anne-Marie in his arms and she was laughing and playing with him. In the short time I have known you she touched my life as well as Suzanne's and I feel privileged to have known her. ..."

Even more unexpected was a letter from Moscow from someone we did not even know: Irina Yuryewa, a friend of my father through his work:

268

"My grief is light........."
A.S. Pushkin

Dear Dimitriy Fyodorovich[13],
The news you told me brought so many feelings and thoughts to the fore, that it was impossible to express them immediately. I am now writing this letter with the big request that you might translate it for Yelisaveta Karlovna[13] and Astrid[13].
The wonderful thing, which happened at the passing of Anne-Marie from this world – they are a sign of hope and comfort both for you and your relations as well as for all who remain on earth.
Always when we grieve for a deceased person, we grieve for ourselves – that someone who was close to us has left us, but at the same time we know that there their soul is at peace and happy, that the Lord, who has overcome death, takes the best souls to himself at a time which is best for them and for all, even though this passing always seems to be premature to us.
The radiance of the divine light – the radiance of Anne-Marie's soul will be with you forever, in your hearts, and it is already awakening in many hearts the spirit of peace, of thankfulness and of love. Without doubt this was an angel who God had sent to earth. And going forth into another world your angel – Anne-Marie, her eternal soul – will support you, help you and console you.
I believe this and will always pray for her soul. My mother expresses her heartfelt sympathy and words of condolence.

May the Lord look after you,
Yours, Irina
12 March 2000

These beautiful words came as a pure blessing to me. How wonderful to think that Anne-Marie was also touching the lives of people who had never met her!

The day after we had come out of hospital with Alma, the first Wednesday after Anne-Marie had died, I saw her for a brief moment. All the members of the Lamb of God Community were sitting in an oval-shaped 'circle' and Larry, the leader of the community, had his right leg crossed over his left. For an instant I saw Anne-Marie making herself quite at home in the centre-space and 'dancing' around the tip of Larry's right shoe. It felt natural and it was nice to see her, if briefly.

At some stage during the first two weeks after Anne-Marie's death, quite without warning, I heard her speaking to me and saying: *"Mummy, would you have me back again?"* I listened with some degree of bewilderment as I answered straight from my heart: "Of course I would, darling, but maybe next time you could be a bit more healthy?" It took me quite some time to come to terms with my answer. I hated to think that I would have put conditions on having her back again, whatever 'having her back again' might actually have meant ...

On the second Monday after Anne-Marie's death when Alma, with her leg in plaster, had to be carried up the stairs in the evening, Pat offered to carry her up but I went ahead anyway. Carrying Alma somewhat awkwardly to the fourth or fifth step, I felt a tear or a rip inside my lower abdomen. I started to bleed heavily. Pat advised me to take a good rest, rather than to spend the night in waiting rooms, only to be sent home again later.

The next morning the GP told me to go to hospital. There a pregnancy test revealed that I had had a miscarriage. It had been very early days, something like eight weeks. I just marvelled about it all. Another little person had come and gone again, surely out of love.

Had this something to do with Anne-Marie's question if I would have her back again? Was she now withdrawing just in order not to come as a sick person again out of love and respect for my wishes? Pondering the mystery of it all while being put on the drip, I thought that there would have been a good chance of complications arising for this little person, had she or he stayed, considering the amount of exposure they had already had to x-rays. I was very aware that *all was well* and that in the midst of all of these unusual normally upsetting occurrences there was the purpose of God who always acted for reasons of purest love.

I was admitted. There was now no more food or drink allowed in case they wanted to operate ("D and C"). I did not want an operation. I had had enough of hospitals, doctors, nurses, drips, fasting, thirsting and arguing a case and I was not relating overly well to the word 'operation.'

It felt as though I was supposed to re-live the experiences of two weeks previously. I had only *one* drip in place and it was limiting all movement of my arm and was very uncomfortable, bordering on being painful. How many drips and lines had Anne-Marie had! How little had I to suffer in comparison with her and what hell she must have gone through with me not even being aware enough to defend her to ensure that she got adequate pain-relief straight away...

I was made to enter into her whole experience again, this time on a new level, re-living a very much toned-down version of her experience in my own body. Had I not appreciated her horrors enough that I should have to be made to enter into them again, now on this level? Maybe that was so. Surely there was a very good reason for all this to happen. This was the third Tuesday in a row that I was spending in hospital. There was something Trinitarian about it.

It was less my actual thirst than the helpless dependence on what 'they' had decided which affected me, as this was one of my most painful memories of Anne-Marie's last day or two, even of up to her last moments. How *could* she understand that Mummy did not give her anything to eat or drink even though she would have so sorely needed it to build up her strength again, which had been wasted on the catheter study...

My poor little darling, dependent on Mummy and Mummy paralysed, unable to see clearly what was needed or unable to act upon her insights and intuition... and Anne-Marie at the receiving end of it, crying out for mercy, and receiving none -- other than that of being taken back to where there is no more hunger, thirst or pain, into the arms of Jesus.

I had been part of the plot and she had not been able even to find any protection or defence in my being there... my empty promises to her... everything welled up within me and wanted to be washed away - and eventually, when the ward-sister came, I found a sympathetic ear and the tears were flowing. Not for the fact that Anne-Marie had died but with pity for the awful time she had had at the end - a time of forsakenness. They were flowing with regret that I had failed her by not being able to make things easier for her and with confusion as to why I was now supposed to relive her experiences albeit in a much milder form.

Maybe I was supposed to get freed of any dread there might have been left of anaesthetics, of operations? One thing was certain: At the speed at which extraordinary events were descending upon me, I did not get a chance to find out whether or not I would have felt the way Dr. Craig had described – wishing things would not just resume their mundane day-to-day routines.

I was pushed to agree to an operation but held out, refusing anything until I had spoken to the consultant Dr. White who was due back in the morning. It was a relief to see him and he wanted to know all about Anne-Marie. Surprised at the joy with which I talked about her, he let me home again so long as we would follow up with outpatient appointments. Thank God.

Isaiah 30 v.20,21: "Although the Lord gives you the bread of adversary and the water of affliction, your teachers will be hidden no more: with your own eyes you will see them. Whether you turn to the right or to the left, your ears will hear a voice behind you, saying "This is the way; walk in it.""

Back home I became aware of how I had been able to get through these weeks of outward turmoil following Anne-Marie's death relatively unflustered. In a dream I saw that when I was walking my feet were resting on those of somebody behind me who was doing all the walking for me. He wore black polished leather shoes and black trousers with an ironed crease. I was held upright by his arms, which were reaching through from under my shoulders and were hooked upwards. I could not see his face but it was like a revelation to know that the strength I had was not my own. I was being carried by the grace of God just like the little reflection "footprints in the sand"[14] so beautifully depicts.

Angela

Raphael brought scarlet fever home from school and it made the rounds in our house. Having lost a lot of blood with the miscarriage, my resistance was low and I became infected, too. From my bed I had been on the phone to one of my friends in Germany for a good hour retelling and re-experiencing a multitude of blessings which had come our way through Anne-Marie. It was very late in the evening and after talking for that length of time I was tired and in need of sleep. I turned over onto my left side and just as I was about to drift into dreamland I heard her voice.

You know how children might taunt each other when brandishing something desirable which is just out of reach of the other? Well that was just how Anne-Marie spoke to me: "*I* know *what* you *nee*-heed." Her tone of voice was anything but welcome at that moment of tiredness and sickness and so, instead of being awestruck or at least amazed, I was ever so slightly irritated by her speaking to me like this at this time.

I said to her that if she knew what I needed maybe she could tell Jesus so that He could give it to me. To my surprise she answered that He had allowed *her* to give it to me! I had to give her the go ahead, even if slightly begrudgingly. I was not feeling up to being playfully handled even though on another level I also liked to know that Anne-Marie was not too far away.

You know the type of giant brushes with very flexible bristles, which are used in automated car wash places – it was this type of thing that Anne-Marie appeared with about a metre and a half above my bed. Its bristles were all hanging downward. They were black with a little white dot on the end of each one. Anne-Marie started 'brushing me down' with this contraption from the place where she was, about a metre and a half above my bed, with none of the bristles actually touching me.

As she was doing this, I felt my fever receding. My temperature was going down noticeably but I still felt tired, very tired, and wanted to sleep, just sleep. Anne-Marie was trying to strike up a conversation with me but it did not go very well. She seemed to be playful and happy and I was just a bit too tired to meet her where she was at. Not really enthralled by all the unusual happenings, I was going to let it go even though Anne-Marie was present. I wanted to sleep.

What I had not noticed was that Our Lord Jesus had been standing by, observing how we got on with each other from a little distance. Seeing that Anne-Marie was not getting very far with me He came over, approaching from my left side wearing a brown garment. Speaking kindly and respectfully to me He said: *"Anne-Marie has asked me the favour of becoming your Guardian Angel."* **(!)**

I had met with Jesus once before, when living an obviously sinful life in England but that time it had been in a dream while fully asleep (November 1986). I had reached the bottom of the barrel and did not know how to go on from there. In this dream we sat next to each other on some knee-height little wall and He was talking with me like a brother. One thing I will never forget about this meeting is His eyes. Eyes like I have never seen on this earth - full of non-judgement and pure love, - He did not mentally slot me into any boxes as we were speaking, not sussing me out, just loving me in the middle of my desolation. I said to Him "I'm in a terrible mess!" and He said to me in a peaceful and friendly way, "You'll get out of it." I answered Him with a tired half- smile "But how?" And He answered me "You'll see, you'll come and follow me."... After that it took nearly two years for this dream to work itself through my system enough to bring about a major change...

This time I was unable to look into his face. I had cast my gaze down onto his cloak. I was too aware of my disrespectful treatment of Anne-Marie when she had tried to strike up a conversation.

Matthew 18 v. 11: "For I tell you that their Angels in Heaven always see the face of my Father in Heaven."

Even if up to then I had not fully taken part in what had been happening around me, when I heard His words spoken to me, all of me realized that this was not just a casual occasion for taking or leaving but a key moment to be lived as fully as possible. I mustered all my inner strength. Thankfulness and appreciation filled me. Inwardly I bowed down low in acceptance of this incredible news. It was an awesome honour.

Anne-Marie then came from up above to sit on my right shoulder. She took off the little slippers she had been buried with and sat on my shoulder with her bare feet dangling forwards, talking with me. I am not sure for how long we were conversing with each other like this - maybe five or ten minutes, but a lot was said.

She told me she would be *in constant view of Our Lord* and that from now on she would *always be on my shoulder*, whether I was aware of it or not. I said to her: "I suppose you'll keep me out of trouble now," and she answered: "*No, Mummy, I can't do that, but I can help you through it.*" She addressed me with "Mummy" every time she addressed me. It seemed strange to me that my own Guardian Angel should address me by calling me 'Mummy' and so I asked her why she was still calling me 'Mummy' but she gave me no answer to this question.

A burning concern of mine had been Kerstin, my goddaughter, my sister's second child over in Germany, who had been suffering from anorexia nervosa for about six months and had reportedly worsened significantly following the death of her little cousin even refusing to eat at all.

I asked Anne-Marie if she could maybe help her in some way and to my astonishment she answered: "Mummy I don't speak any German." I could not believe what I heard and responded in disbelief, saying that this sort of thing should not matter anymore now that she was in the heavenly realms. (How imposturous of me to think that I should know better about these things than her!) She graciously overlooked my comment and said that the only thing that she could do for Kerstin was to ask Our Lord himself to help her.

She also probingly mentioned that I had let her go quite lightly. This was a sore topic for me as I had wondered about this myself. It was irritating me. I acknowledged that she was right and started to be remorseful about it when she reassured me, saying that it had been completely right this way.

We talked about other things as well and she was highly amused at my enquiring if it was okay for me to turn round and lie on my right side, wondering if I would squash her if I came to rest on the shoulder she was sitting on. She assured me that that sort of thing could not harm her anymore.

I was by now lying on my right side, still in conversation with her, when from somewhere out there an avalanche of contorted grimaces and strange and hideous little beings came rolling on towards us, more specifically *her*, at great speed. There had been no warning of this and initially I was not reacting in any way to try to help to avert this onslaught. One noticeable feature of this train of unpleasant looking creatures was that even though it seemed to be aimed at us, it was not able to touch us. Instead, it rolled by Anne-Marie without harming her in any way.

After a moment or two I understood it as an angry reaction of the powers of darkness to the newly established changed circumstances of Anne-Marie coming to be my Guardian Angel. Even though they were not able to touch us it was still not a very pleasant experience and so I decided to sing praises to God (even if quietly, as it was by now the middle of the night) to dispel any darkness.

When the situation had passed Anne-Marie remarked that they would be back at some future point. I suppose it is good to be warned. Our time of unhindered conversation was coming to an end. The whole momentous experience had left me energised, with my fever gone and ready to get up and be well.

I went downstairs where my darling Pat was still sitting up at the kitchen table, finishing his day with his prayers even though it was after one o'clock at night. I told him that I had just received a bit of healing; and that at this time of the night! He very wisely answered that surely any time of the day or night was a good time to get well again and welcomed me to sit down by the kitchen table.

Somehow I was now too awake and energised to go back to bed and stayed up even after he had gone, reading in my bible and marvelling at the things I had experienced. It was hard to believe that only a little while ago all this had taken place and now it was all over; that only a little while ago I was too tired and sick to be thinking of getting up and that now I was feeling energised and well. There was of course also the niggling suspicion that my brain had been playing tricks with me. After all, having a fever might very well cause 'funny' things to happen. I had not measured my temperature to be able to accurately say how high it might have been but I was sure that it had, at any rate, not been dangerously high.

A memory came to my aid. Flooding back with strength it helped me to hold on to my blessings, to the graces I had received, not allowing them to be taken away by the eternal twister, liar and thief. It was the memory of the Thursday before Anne-Marie's operation, when I had been immersed in singing praise with the Siloam Community (now 'John the Baptist Community') and had received something invisible which I had gently guided to come to rest on my right shoulder. I had felt it as a privilege and blessing at the time. It had been a preview of what was to come to pass. Now the memory of it confirmed what had happened here and now.

I took note and decided more firmly not to allow myself to be robbed of my blessings but to hold on to them, to treasure them and to praise God in doing so. Had Our Lord not been tried after his Baptism? Had the tempter not tried to cause Him to forfeit *all* through cunning deceit? How important to be vigilant and to hold on to faith rather than being out-manoeuvred and robbed of one's destiny and life.

Anne-Marie had assured me that she would be there even if I was not aware of it. She had said that she was going to be in constant view of Our Lord. Surely both those statements were truly momentous in their reach and realm, permeating all of any future I might have left to live from that point onwards. She had become my Guardian Angel; she had become what I had sensed about her when I had chosen her middle name: Angela.

Jeremiah 6 v.16: "Stand at the crossroads and look: ask for the ancient paths, ask where the good way is, and walk in it, and you will find rest for your souls."

Into the Future

Over seven years have passed since Anne Marie became my Guardian Angel and she continues to involve herself in our lives. I am sure she had something to do with us receiving our 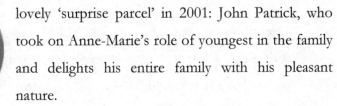 lovely 'surprise parcel' in 2001: John Patrick, who took on Anne-Marie's role of youngest in the family and delights his entire family with his pleasant nature.

We have without doubt also been helped by her prayers and by the path she caused me to take on our journey through six months of chemotherapy for Pascal's Hodgkin's disease. He is now 14 years of age and presently 'in remission'. Please, Anne-Marie, continue to intercede.

The path Anne-Marie opened up for me led me into Orthodoxy. Her coming through a Russian Orthodox icon re-awakened my old love of the Russian Orthodox Church, which I had when I was a girl. Listening with my father to his records of Orthodox choir music I had found it full of depth, peace and longsuffering beauty. I now see this as springing from a wealth of profound spiritual truth. Even then it had brought to my mind the imagery of a majestic broad and deep river, which, sure of its destiny, flowed to the sea with dignity, austerity and peace. It touched parts in me which nothing else was able to reach.

At about fifteen years of age I experienced an Orthodox Easter Celebration which stayed with me through time for the authenticity of the outpouring of joy from the members of the congregation. I saw their eyes shining, their joy written on their faces and can nearly still feel the hugs they gave me even though I knew not one of them.

Intermittently over the years I have had pangs of longing for the Orthodox Church. On one occasion I even travelled to Corfu to try to see if it would be possible to move there for the sake of the Church. Shortly before Anne-Marie's birth I had made arrangements with an Orthodox priest in Dublin: I would travel down to him every Saturday in order to have a series of chats. But with Anne-Marie so ill, this did not come to pass.

Instead, the Orthodox Church arrived in Belfast. I went to a newly established Orthodox study group, where Geoffrey Ready, a Canadian Orthodox Deacon, opened up worlds of depth of Tradition, faith and worship. This was something I had been craving for years and it was a relief to be tutored.

When Lieta (R.I.P.), the Capozona (head of the zone) for Ireland of the Focolare Movement at that time heard of this, she said: "See, how God loves you!", and indeed, it has been an immeasurable blessing to me. I have found within the bosom of this ancient Church and mother of all Christian Churches, what I had sensed so many years previously: Depth, serenity, longsuffering humility, lucid spiritual truth and knowledge, peace and joy, a real taste of the immeasurable love of God, a profound sense of belonging and as such a place for growth.

I have found a wealth of very valuable and sacred signposts, Spirit-bearers, in place to help the searching earthling enter ever more deeply into the all-important relationship with God, which has the definite potential to transform every aspect of life towards the final goal of theosis, of being filled with, inhabited by and at one with God. There are the Scriptures, the Sacraments, the Icons, the Church-fathers, the Saints... There is such a richness of tools to use!

What relief, too, to see life as a *developing path*, supported by and interwoven with the Church. The Church, who assists us in our frailty to re-orientate ourselves by means of both repentance and confession, sets us free from the bondage of sin. It continually draws on Christ's Mercy when accompanying the meditative and enlightening journey inward to find our mournful condition of fallenness in oh so many aspects of our lives... continually helping us to try to overcome more of our inbuilt resistance to holiness by the Spirit of God.

Isaiah 43 v1: "Fear not, for I have redeemed you; I have summoned you by name; you are mine."

And although I had loved the Orthodox Church for a very long time from a distance, I found myself strangely unsure about entering into it. It is an Orthodox custom to take on a new name upon entry into the Church, (unless one wanted to confirm a Christian name already given) although not everyone would make this new name their main name. I had no doubt which name to take but it seemed strange at 40 years of age to start using another name.

Yet, this was my opportunity to unite my childhood knowledge with the present times. My parents still remember that during childhood I had repeatedly insisted that they had given me the wrong name and that I should have been called Johanna. This name had now become very meaningful. It is the German female form for Johannes, John. It took Anne-Marie to come in his spirit, to prepare the way and to open my eyes to my patron Saint.

Still, when I was about to become a Catechumen – i.e. an officially received learner and listener in preparation for becoming a full church member - on 9 December 2000, I felt like a somewhat unsure outsider looking in. How reassuring, therefore, to hear the Lord speak to me just moments before the part of the Service during which I was to become a Catechumen began: *"Johanna, - you are mine."* Everything was confirmed - both the choice of my name and the direction I had taken - and my joy was overflowing.

Towards the end of 2001, when I had been a Catechumen for about a year, the question about becoming a full member of the Orthodox Church was becoming evermore insistent and had to be addressed. There are basically two ways of entry. One is by baptism and the other by Chrismation (exclusively for already baptised believers).

Philippians 4 v. 7: "And the peace of God, which transcends all understanding, will guard your hearts and your minds in Christ Jesus."

I wrestled with and rebelled against the idea of re-baptism proposed by my Archbishop as I did not want to make a statement of declaring the baptisms of other Christian churches as void. It took a lot of time and prayer, but eventually there was a breakthrough experience.

While at prayer in front of my icon of the Lord, I received a great Peace about being baptised. This went 100 per cent against everything I thought I grasped with my understanding but was compelling. It was helped along during the Service for 19 January 2002, of 'The Baptism of Our Lord', when I could not escape the truth that Our Lord himself would not have needed to be baptised but went ahead reasoning (Matthew 3v.14 &15): *"Let it be so now; it is proper for us to do this to fulfil all righteousness."* None of my reasoning could stand up against such humility.

At prayer in the Lamb of God community some time later, when I was laying face-down, I heard the Lord speak to me. *"Get up! I have made you in my image and likeness."* I got up and sat down again on my chair. *"About your baptism…"* 'Yes, Lord?'… *'I want you to be baptized…'* 'I know…' *"…in the river Jordan."* This was momentous! I asked for confirmation of this and at the very same meeting two people made contributions about the river Jordan and its significance. Thus the question was reduced to "When?"

With this question as yet unanswered I accepted an invitation by my father (Dad) to visit Russia for the first time. In the summer of 2002, my father (79 at that time) my sister, her son and I were part of a group of Germans travelling on a package-trip around the 'Golden Ring', a number of very old Russian Orthodox towns and cities in the heart of Russia.

A friend from Switzerland rang the day before take-off. She had *just by chance* come across an old address of a certain Fr. Andrei Logvinov. Of all the people she had come in contact with, when she had been in Kostroma - one of the cities of the Golden Ring - some ten years previously, it had been this man, this priest, who had impressed her most.

First we visited Moscow (July - Oh what heat!), where my father and I separated ourselves from our group in order to visit the Rublyov Museum where the original of "Anne-Marie's" *St John the Baptist Icon* is kept. The museum was closed but after hearing about Anne-Marie, the guard eventually allowed us in. Two very interested ladies took us to the room where it was hanging with its counterpart, the icon of Our Lady, one on either side of a wide doorway.

Thanks to my father's interpreting skills, the museum ladies got to hear a summary of Anne-Marie's story. They were captivated, eagerly affirming that they would tell this story to the visitors of the museum. Quite possibly, if the museum had been open, nobody might have heard about the wonders... another God-event...

I spent a little time in the presence of the icon. – Both spiritually and colour-wise it looked a little lighter to me than on our prints. The touch of nearly a breath of pink on the 'frame', which was only partially visible on my print at home, seemed to lighten it. ... There was *joy* with the gravity of St.John! ... Glory to God.

I had wanted to see the original of "Anne-Marie's icon" before. I had thought of visiting it as a pilgrimage, quite convinced that it would be a wonderful thing to do until, full of these thoughts, I gazed over to my icon and felt a stern pulling-up! *Did I really think that the things which had happened* [through my copy of the original] *were counterfeit?*

I had to acknowledge that the spiritual truth conveyed through my copy was in no way inferior to any which would be carried by the 'original'. Having fully understood this, the visit to the museum was free of idolatry and therefore a great blessing.

Our journey around the Golden Ring of Orthodox cities in the heart of Russia eventually took us to Kostroma. This is quite a major city of about 300 000 inhabitants situated along the banks of the majestic river Volga. Yet the only two people we asked in different locations about directions or contact details for Fr.

Andrei Logvinov both immediately knew him. …enough incredible stories here for a separate little booklet!

Unable to reach him by telephone, my father and I set out to try to visit Fr. Andrei after our evening meal on our first of two nights in Kostroma. At his green wooden house at the other end of town there was no answer, but a string of 'coincidences' so finely affected the timing of our return journey, that we encountered Fr Andrei for a timeless few minutes at the tram stop where we were waiting to return to our hotel.

I addressed this bearded man who was walking with a joyful bounce towards the street where his house was, with a querying "Fr. Andrei??" Fr. Andrei later referred to this meeting as 'a miracle'. Speaking with him, I was surrounded by something of an extraordinary bubble of unity, of joy, of timelessness, of blessing. When the tram we had been waiting for came, he quickly reassured us to take it, saying - in perfect English - that they did not come very frequently.

Fr. Andrei was standing by, on the other side of the closing glass doors, blessing us…with a blessing so rich, so real, so joyful in its outworking that I was floating back through Kostroma in this tram, my heart overflowing.

The people on the tram, their plight, their heartaches, their problems, were inescapable, insistent, compelling. I wanted to tell them all: "There *is* hope, there *is* joy, there *is* meaning to your lives,

God *really does love every one of you*, He really *does* care..." but while I saw *them*, they did not seem to see me or to notice my state of blessedness.

Father Andrei, this deeply humble and simultaneously joyful man, is unobtrusively alive to every moment, ready to help and encourage everybody of whatever age. This saintly man came to visit us here after Easter 2003. - By this time I had become a full member of the Orthodox Church. - He left a blessing presence and memories of *countless* touching encounters with holiness. He conducted a service of 'Blessing of the Grave' at Anne-Marie's grave while big white clouds were speeding across the blue sky. There it became obvious to both of us that *she* had had a major part in our connection and in his coming over to Belfast.

The Russian trip and my first encounter with the poet-priest-saint had confirmed my direction beyond doubt and after much discernment of the correct timing of my baptism, the feast of the 'Baptism of Our Lord' (19 January 2003), stood out as the obvious choice. Plans were made and tickets bought.

Near the time of departure, when I rang up to confirm arrangements, the head of the mission on the Mount of Olives, Fr. Andronik, asked me if I would mind very much if (for reasons beyond his control) my baptism was delayed by one day. He reminded me, that the feast of the Lord's Baptism is celebrated for a number of days anyway and added that 20 January is also the synaxis (related feast celebrated the day after a major feast day) of St *John the Baptist*. (!) Did I need any more confirmation?

When the person I had arranged to travel with cancelled due to safety fears amid the very unstable circumstances in Israel, I still had no doubt that I was supposed to go ahead even if this meant travelling on my own. I did and the blessings flowed freely.

There are two Russian Orthodox monasteries on the Mount of Olives. These two monasteries organise an annual trip to the river Jordan taking two bus loads of nuns to be present and to sing at the annual service of baptism of new converts. In the year 2003 this annual trip had been postponed by one day because of the arrival of an important Bishop...

Within the grounds of the convent on top of the Mount of Olives where I was staying at first, there is a small chapel dedicated to *St. John the Baptist*. This chapel is opened only on *his* feast-days. The day of departure to the Jordan River was the Synaxis feast of St. John the Forerunner, and so we had the five o'clock morning service in this, his chapel, in the presence no less of one of his relics – a tiny peace of his head.

Once on the way I remembered that I had promised a number of people some Jordan water but that I had forgotten to bring a container for this. I wondered how I could remedy this situation when we pulled up for a break en route. The backdoors of the bus opened and on the ground in front of me I found a large empty water bottle *with its lid in place*...

We were joined by a group of six other candidates - four adults and two children - for baptism by triple full immersion at a well established baptismal area of the Jordan River.

It was January, raining and cold, but the coldness of the river Jordan did not register with me when I was being baptised. I did not begin to feel cold until quite a lot later, towards the end of the service. One nun excitedly reported back to me that at the time of my baptism a bird had flown over me, twice.

After the baptisms we went on to Lake Galilee into a church where everybody stood singing in beautiful harmonies. I stood among everybody else in the church, immersed in the singing which absolutely filled the church, with tears rolling down my cheeks. I was now no longer looking in from the outside. I was now at one. …. I had become part of the ancient Orthodox Church …..

Thank you, God and thank you, Anne-Marie, my Guardian Angel, for your part in this.

I took a solitary stroll to the lakeshore of Lake Galilee and came to a wooden picnic-table. Sitting down on one of the attached benches I was taking in a peaceful lakeside scene. To my left, at the head of the table, there was an old chair, the back of which was hanging down at an angle from one rusty nail. I became intensely aware of the Lord's Presence on this chair. I could *see* nothing out of the ordinary but I *felt* His presence. Before long He said, in a very friendly and interested sort-of way: *"Well, did you have a nice day?"*

It still puts a smile on my face to think of it now. It was only when I proceeded to tell him all the events of the day, beginning with the five o'clock service in St. John the Baptist's chapel right through to the then present time that I became aware of the immense and innumerable blessings I had received this day.

... As I was leaving He called me: *"Johanna -?"*
I turned back and looked at the old rusty chair.   *"Yes, Lord?"*
With a little smile in His voice, He said: *"I love you!"*
My joyful answer was not long in coming – *"I love you, too!"*

There had been a question over my receiving my first Holy Communion, as the convent I was staying in had the tradition of abstaining from it during women's monthly flow, and I had informed them that this was my position. My new godmother, Sr. Vera, a nun of the convent at the base of the Mount of Olives, sought to obtain permission for me, and while there seemed to be some excitement and concern among the nuns, I was sure everything had happened by appointment and did not mind if I had to wait for my first Holy Communion until I would return to Belfast.

In the convent one would prepare for receiving the Eucharist in the morning by going to the evening service, the day before. During the evening service before my last morning in the Holy Land, my godmother came over to me and informed me that

I had been granted permission to receive the Eucharist in the morning. I was not very responsive as I had been immersed in the presence of God and had not felt the lack of anything. Sr. Vera asked me to pray about it.

Eventually I went to the main part of the church, not yet having homed in on any specific prayer. My gaze fell upon the icon of our Lord on the iconostasis. [*Separation between altar area and main body of church*] He was depicted seated, wearing a white robe. With a kindly voice He said to me, *"You're coming, aren't you?"* As He spoke I became deeply aware that if I was to deny this invitation I would be turning my back on *everything* he had done for me and that it was not only a well-meaning priest or nun who had invited me to His Eucharist but My Lord Himself.

I received Holy Communion and came out of the church overlooking Jerusalem from the Mount of Olives in the early morning. My feet were rooted. My tears were flowing. I was speechless.

Afterword

Back in our parish here, I am now a full member and at home. My hope is that within the bosom of this rich and ancient Church by God's Grace and Mercy His Spirit will continue to guide me - directly and with the help of His Angels and Saints, priests and people (including my faithful daughter, friend and angel Anne-Marie) - into an ever deeper knowledge and love of Him and my neighbour and will also enable my heart to become ever more responsive to His guidance.

Anne-Marie continues to involve herself in life on earth from the heavenly realm. Many remarkable things have happened and continue to happen. There was the advertising campaign of the love of God on North-Belfast buses,[15] and the building of a garden chapel[16] as well as the charity shop.[17] Anne-Marie's involvement continues to be evident in small details[18] as well as on the larger scale, such as the publication of a local monthly North Belfast magazine, serialising her story, which brought with it its own wonders... so in many ways, this book is necessarily incomplete[19].

It is a little strange, too, to write about everything that happened without knowing you, the reader, personally. Although unworthy of the comparison through my endless failings, I feel united with Mary in giving my child to you and into the world. Like her Son and like all the Saints, Anne-Marie did not only come for her own immediate family and friends but for the encouragement of all of us to hold out, to obediently live out our own unique yet universal calling for our own fulfilment, for the benefit of others, and for the Glory of God.

Thank you, Anne-Marie and

Glory to God,

Amen.

NB
May 2015: Anne-Marie has had an influence on many people's lives and a number of people believe to have had answers to their prayers through her intercession.
There may well be an enquiry into this in the future, with a view to making her more generally known. So please do not be shy in contacting me at johanna.mcbride@btinternet.com if you have some information to add to this enquiry.
Many thanks, and may God bless you,
Johanna

Matthew 11, v.14-15 "And if you are willing to accept it, he is the Elijah who was to come. He who has ears, let him hear."

Epilogue
(Written in 2007)

Now, nearly ten years after Anne-Marie came to join us, with the distance of time from the day-to-day events of her coming and going, a greater consciousness is dawning.

Not only have I had thoughts on the meaning of *'the heart'* as a most essential thing, and of new ways to try to understand Anne-Marie's heart[20], but - in accordance with Dr Craig's tentative suggestion that we may find her story will continue to unfold - it is also beginning to become clearer that Anne-Marie's life is not just a remarkable blessed story. Her coming by announcement through the icon of St John the Baptist, (St John the Forerunner) is more than a wondrous event leading me to Orthodoxy.

At the time of Anne-Marie's conception there was no Orthodox Church in Northern Ireland, whereas now, there is a vibrant international Orthodox Community. Anne-Marie not only opened the doors of her mother's consciousness to the reverberating and humbling beauty and depth of the mother of all Christian Churches, but, true to the spirituality of St John as the Preparer of the Way, the one who said "He *[Jesus]* must increase, but I must decrease" (John 3:30) I believe now, that Anne-Marie was also instrumental in the Spiritual Realm in bringing about the arrival (or *revival* after centuries of its absence) of Orthodoxy in Northern Ireland.

Like St John the Baptist, The Forerunner, who was killed before the birth of the Christian Church, Anne-Marie did not live to see the Orthodox Church become a sacramental community. At the time of her passing the deacon who started the mission here had not yet been made priest.

The Church is now in place just in time for welcoming - apart from you and me - also the many "Cradle-Orthodox" Christians who are arriving from Eastern European and many other countries these days, reminding us of the universal nature of the original faith of the apostles as preserved without change by the Orthodox Church.

If you were touched by Anne-Marie's story, I believe you will also be blessed by paying a visit to the Orthodox Church here in Belfast[21], or wherever you happen to live.

Be encouraged to seek God.

May the Lord bless you.

Glory to God!
Amen.

Anne-Marie November '99

P.S. If you would like to contact me you can email me on
johanna.mcbride@btinternet.com

Appendix

F ootnotes

1. Icons are pictures of holy people widely used in Christian Orthodox Tradition to help prayer and advancement of faith in our triune God. Both the icons mentioned here were originally from Pskov in the North-West of Russia and the originals are now kept in the Rubljov Museum in Moscow.

   For people with difficulty regarding the concept of icons it may be useful to think of a photograph of a person you love. Most likely the reason you like to look at the photograph is because it puts you in mind of this person...Even should you find yourself giving a wee kiss to the photograph, it is the person who is depicted, who you intend as the receiver of it, not the piece of paper.

2. The *"Word of Life"* is a monthly reflection written until recent times by Chiara Lubich, the leader and founder of the Focolare movement (see footnote 3). In it a short reading from scriptures is explored as to its practical implications for our lives.

3. The Focolare movement is a worldwide movement. Its beginnings lay in Italy at the end of the Second World War. The movement tries to implement the Gospel in day-to-day living. It has its own website. www.rc.net/focolare It has grown far beyond the borders of the Catholic Church within which it originated, but has maintained strong links with it.

4. The Lamb of God Community is a community of committed people of different Christian backgrounds, who meet regularly on a Wednesday evening at 8pm in Shalom House on the Cliftonville Road. in Belfast. (everyone welcome!)

5. The "Alpha" course is a course in basic Christianity. It is using a small group structure and was designed for our present times by Nicky Gumble, a minister in the Anglican Church. More information via   www.alphacourse.org

6. "Shalom House" a Community Centre owned by the Lamb of God Community. (Footnote 4) Cliftonville Road .North Belfast

7. For more information on Vassula and her ministry see her "True Life in God" website: www.tlig.org

8. The Heartbeat Northern Ireland Charity is a Parent Support Group for families of children who have heart disease. You can find their website at www.heartbeatni.co.uk

9. The Munich MacDonald's House is one of many such facilities worldwide, built by the pennies which those going for quick meals at this chain have dropped into the transparent house-shaped collection boxes.

10. Zivis (Zivil Dienst Leistende) are young German men who either refused or who were deemed medically unfit to serve in the army, and are required by law to serve the country in other ways instead, such as in hospitals or social institutions.

11. You can find out more about the Koinonia Giovanni Battista at their website www.koinoniagb.org.

12. Embalming is not, as I initially assumed, referring to externally applied lotions or potions but instead involves, as one essential feature, the removal of the blood of the deceased – under pressure - and the replacement of this blood by a preservative chemical. Quite apart from other, to my mind questionable and often more variable details, such as emptying the bowel contents, sewing up the lips, and packing the nose against leakage etc., the thought of a body being pumped full of chemicals instead of containing its own blood feels like sacrilege to me.

In the course of my enquiries I asked if it was possible to bury the person's blood with them in a container in their coffin, but was told that this would not be possible, as their blood was passed on to a chemical factory. I knew enough to steer clear of embalming if or when death was to visit our family.

13. My father's Russian friends address him by the name 'Dimitriy Fyodorovych', while 'Yelisaveta Karlovna' is referring to my mother, - Elisabeth, daughter of Karl. Finally 'Astrid' was the name I was known by before I changed my name to 'Johanna' (pronounced Yohanna) on entering into the Orthodox Church.

14. "Footprints in the sand" different versions of this well known poem can be found on the following website: http://www.wowzone.com/fprints.htm

15. In August 2001, with John Patrick only a number of months old, I lay awake one night with an ever more strongly burning idea of advertising the love of God on the busses here in Belfast. Money from a maturing life insurance was due in February of 2002, so I decided that the run up to Easter would be an obvious time for such a campaign.
By means of a string of incredible blessed "coincidences" and prayer support this campaign went ahead. What an extra bonus to find the head of the advertising company to be a lay preacher and committed Christian, who offered to double the length of the campaign at no extra cost for me!

For some weeks the buses travelled through mainly North Belfast displaying Francesca's (John Patrick's Italian graphic designer godmother) beautifully gentle artwork, saying things like "Yes, it's true, God loves you – even now" on the outside while inside the reading of the prodigal son was displayed on the separation wall between the driver and passengers. The much bigger, nationwide 'Power to Change' campaign had been postponed to run in the autumn and this gave our little campaign a St. John the Forerunner feel, preparing the way.

16. Our garden church

During time spent immersed in prayer, the Lord had directed me to build an Orthodox Chapel in our back garden. A wooden log cabin was erected and has turned into a beautiful little Orthodox church, blessed and dedicated to St. John the Baptist nearly a year later, on Sunday, 9 March 2003, the day after Anne-Marie's anniversary if one takes this to be the 8 March (rather than Ash Wednesday). It was also the beginning of "Great Lent" (the name of the Orthodox fasting period in the run-up to Easter) and therefore the nearest one could get to 'Ash Wednesday' within the Orthodox setting.

[The Orthodox way of entering into the preparation for Easter on this day is by a beautiful annual Service of Forgiveness, where *every* person present approaches *every* other person to ask for, and receive forgiveness.]

17. The Charity Shop has connections to Elisha, Elijah and St. John the Baptist: Spiritually speaking, the beginnings of the shop extend back to Sunday 27 June 1999, and the Old Testament reading of the day in the Catholic Church was 2 Kings chapter 4 verse 11-16:

One day Elisha went to Shunem. And a well-to-do woman was there, who urged him to stay for a meal. So whenever he came by, he stopped there to eat. She said to her husband, "I know that this man who often comes our way is a holy man of God. Let's make a small room on the roof and put in it a bed and a table, a chair and a lamp for him. Then he can stay there whenever he comes to us."
One day when Elisha came, he went up to his room and lay down there. He said to his servant Gehazi, "Call the Shunammite." So he called her and she stood before him. Elisha said to him, "Tell her, 'You have gone to all this trouble for us. Now what can be done for you? Can we speak on your behalf to the king or the commander of the army?'" She replied, "I have a home among my own people."
"What can be done for her?" Elisha asked. Gehazi said, "Well, she has no son and her husband is old." Then Elisha said, "Call her." So he called her, and she stood in the doorway. "About this time next year," Elisha said, "you will hold a son in your arms."

This reading hit me very forcibly. So much so, that when I heard it read, I was sitting with tears streaming down my face. I knew it was for me, but did not really know what it was to mean.

Quite some time later, during a chat with the leader of the Columbanus Community (this has since made way for the Irish School of Ecumenics) Rev. Glen Barkley opened my eyes to understanding 'the shop' as a spiritual child of mine. This was confirmed by the fact, that our opening date, the feast-day of St. John the Baptist, the 24 June (according to the Western calendar), was truly "about this time next year".

It struck me quite intensely that the prophet Elisha, on the occasion of the departure of the prophet Elijah had received a double portion of his spirit (2 Kings 2, v.7-15):

Fifty men of the company of the prophets went and stood at a distance, facing the place where Elijah and Elisha had stopped at the Jordan. Elijah took his cloak, rolled it up and struck the water with it. The water divided to the right and to the left, and the two of them crossed over on dry ground. When they had crossed, Elijah said to Elisha, "Tell me, what can I do for you before I am taken from you?" "Let me inherit a double portion of your spirit," Elisha replied. "You have asked a difficult thing," Elijah said, "Yet if you see me when I am taken from you, it will be yours—otherwise not." As they were walking along and talking together, suddenly a chariot of fire and horses of fire appeared and separated the two of them, and Elijah went up to heaven in a whirlwind. Elisha saw this and cried out, "My father! My father! The chariots and horsemen of Israel!" And Elisha saw him no more. Then he took hold of his own clothes and tore them apart. He picked up the cloak that had fallen from Elijah and went back and stood on the bank of the Jordan. Then he took the cloak that had fallen from him and struck the water with it. "Where now is the Lord, the God of Elijah?" he asked. When he struck the water, it divided to the right and to the left, and he crossed over. The company of the prophets from Jericho who were watching said "The spirit of Elijah is resting on Elisha..."

And as according to Our Lord Jesus Christ St. John the Baptist was Elijah, (Matthew11 v.7-15):

Jesus began to speak to the crowd about John: "...... This is the one about whom it is written: " 'I will send my messenger ahead of you, who will prepare your way before you.' I tell you the truth: Among those born of women there has not risen anyone greater than John the Baptist; yet he who is least in the kingdom of heaven is greater than he. From the days of John the Baptist until now, the kingdom of heaven has been forcefully advancing, and forceful men lay hold of it. For all the Prophets and the Law prophesied until John. And if you are willing to accept it, he is the Elijah who was to come. He who has ears, let him hear."

this points to a very strong connection between the three powerful prophets Elijah, Elisha and St. John the Baptist who were all active at the river Jordan.

All three were evidently involved with our family; Elijah by causing me to take food on my journey through the desert, when he came to mind at that junction, Elisha in bringing about the shop, and of course St. John the Baptist was the preparer of the way, through whom Anne-Marie had come...

The shop flourished and fulfilled its purpose for about two and a half years, gaining charitable status under the name of "Come and See". [...A name intended to span the whole experience of the Christian life: *on the one hand* it is Christ's invitation to be with Him - when St. John's disciples had asked Our Lord "where do you live?"- and *on the other hand* it was Lazarus's sister's invitation towards Christ to come to us, to where *we* are (in the tomb) - when Jesus had asked her about her brother Lazarus: "Where have you laid him?" It also seemed an unassuming name for anyone not aware of these scriptures, which would sound friendly and inviting.]

After the arrival of our youngest, John Patrick, and after prayerful consideration I closed the shop until further notice – I am very aware of the Shumanite woman's son dying at some later stage, only to be brought back to life by Elisha. In likewise manner, the money from the sale of the shop has helped to support the beginnings of Orthodoxy in Northern Ireland, to publish a monthly BT15 magazine serialising Anne-Marie's story, and to publish this manuscript. Thus my spiritual child is not only resurrected, but is purposefully living for others.

18. Examples of "smaller" Anne-Marie-events:

Jess

Anne-Marie had died on Ash-Wednesday. This being a rather special day in the preparation for Easter-time, I had since then wondered what unusual thing might happen for Easter. The answer came in the form of the surprise arrival of an abandoned dog at the farm in Co. Tyrone, where Pat was busy with the lambing season. A lovely collie-cross dog arrived. Extensive research as to his rightful owner yielded no results - so we kept him.

Isaiah 11, v.6: " ...the wolf will live with the lamb..."

Jess was a friendly dog, and when Pat brought a little lamb that needed to be bottle-fed, home to our back garden in Belfast, the dog and the lamb made friends, and would sleep curled up next to each other. This felt like an extra special blessing to me, fulfilling Isaiah's prophecy regarding the signs that will accompany the presence of the Lord.

Cemetery

One day in the weeks after Anne-Marie's passing when I seemed to have immeasurably more time than before, I decided to spend the half hour before going to a prayer group at Anne-Marie's grave-side. It was summertime, and the graveyard was open late.

I was driving into the graveyard on this lovely summer evening, singing praise songs, looking forward to a bit of time, spent homing in on Anne-Marie. I was surprised to hear her little voice, saying to me: "You know, of course, that I'm not here, Mummy". I answered her and said that I still thought that it would be nice to keep her little plot nice in memory of her, but she did not say anything else in response.

"Angels- I'm one"

A good friend of mine who had known Anne-Marie well, phoned up with this little story about two years after Anne-

Marie had died. Apparently she had been sitting on the bed of her teenage daughter at bedtime chatting about a few things with her. In the course of the conversation her daughter asked her outright if she believed in angels. On a different day she may well have said something different, but as it happened she said: "No. – I've never seen one." Instantly, her daughter pleaded with great concern, "Mummy, what's wrong? Are you all right?" She had seen her mother's face change from chatty to pale, with a half-open mouth. My friend described what had happened like this: "Just as the words had left my lips, I felt a little slap on one of my cheeks and heard distinctively Anne-Marie's voice saying "I'm one!" Her daughter persuaded her to share this story with me.

The Pendant

On one of her visits to us, Reyes, Alma's Spanish godmother, had brought with her a fine golden chain with a little golden pendant with her for Alma and another one for Anne-Marie. Both girls wore their presents for a while until the chains broke. I had put Anne-Marie's pendant in a ring-box and had not thought any further about it, until I discovered it again, a year or two later, on my own birthday in June 2000.

It seemed as if Anne-Marie was giving me a birthday present of her pendant, and now for the first time the pendant made sense to me. On the face of this half inch round golden pendant, a little child-angel is engraved. Around it, written in Spanish, there are the words "I watch over you". Her name, "Anne-Marie", on the reverse of it, in fine handwriting script, read like her signature that day.

Three flowers, three animals

Going steadily onwards, with Anne-Marie's physical presence further and further in the past, some flowers and some animals have the ability of bringing her to mind.

The flowers:

a.   the pink rose, as our pink rosebush in front of our window in the front garden was laden with fragrant pink roses when we first came home after she was born, as never before or since; (there are two on her grave now)

b.   the sunflower, as she was our sunshine, and as she had been given a lovely summer sunflower dress, which she had worn practically all of her best summer 1999 and as Sharon used to light a sunflower candle for her;

c.   the bluebell, or even more specifically the white bluebell, as that was how Fr. McBride had so befittingly described her. (There are plenty on her grave now)

The animals:

a.   the ladybird, as this came to me in the middle of winter to encourage me in Munich;

b.   the butterfly, as Pascal had endearingly called her our butterfly, as she was so slight and light, and used to wear a butterfly clip in her hair; and

c.   the penguin, as this was her favourite animal depicted also on her last drawings in Birmingham, and as she had an insatiable appetite for spending her time in the water.

Of the animals - the penguin - has the foremost position, even though both butterflies and ladybirds have appeared in unusual or meaningful situations, such as the time when all of her grave was covered with ladybirds, while even upon careful inspection, none could be found anywhere else in the vicinity...

...or when one of our children was sitting on the path that led up to Granny's house, crying because of something that had been said and a butterfly came and flew all around him, until he had to smile again... (*and*, about half an hour after writing this passage a friend who was not aware of these things came by, bringing me for no apparent reason a present in a little cardboard box: a beautiful two-and-a-half inch delicately painted fine cloth butterfly. - Call it coincidence?)

The penguin (a squeaky plastic one, whose appearance has as yet remained unexplained, turned up on the side of our bath) has become something of a trademark for her making her presence known at any important time, but notably especially during holiday times, where penguins just appear in form of toys, stickers, children's rub-off tattoos etc.

However, the most striking of incidents would have to be the unusual congratulations card we got from our neighbour Monika on the occasion of the baptism of Anne-Marie's younger brother, John Patrick. Monika was not aware of the significance of the appearance of penguins to our family, but wrote her sentiments on a card depicting a penguin on the front. Her gift, a little crystal owl, felt like a greeting from our good friend Libby (R.i.P.), a formerly dedicated collector of owls of just about the same size as the one given to us. To me it felt, as though we had received congratulations from both Anne-Marie and Libby on the occasion of John Patrick's baptism, and I nearly forgot to thank Monika!

Keeping in touch

On birthdays and special occasions there was a noticeable connection with Anne-Marie simply via meeting or hearing from someone of her name especially for the first three years after her death.

For the first three years after Anne-Marie's death we also committed almost every Wednesday evening to a family get together, sometimes also with visitors, and/or neighbours, for a little prayer service at which we sang the songs and read the readings of her funeral Mass. This enabled her readings (see "The day of the Funeral") to become anchored in our hearts and there to start to unfold their mission.

19. More experiences accumulate. If you have a story to tell, of how Anne-Marie maybe touched you, or even helped you in one way or another, please feel free to contact me. Who knows? Perhaps there might be a follow-up at some later stage. (Email: johanna.mcbride@btinternet.com)

20. An after-thought to ponder: Anne-Marie's heart. The bigger pumping chamber in the normal heart pumps the blood around the body. The smaller pumping chamber pumps the blood into the lungs for refreshing.
In Anne-Marie's heart this was reversed. The bigger pumping chamber pumped her used blood to the lungs, and the smaller one pumped her blood around her body.

*Isaiah 57:16 "I will not accuse forever, nor will I always be angry, for then the spirit of man would grow faint before me — the **breath** of man that I have created."*

If we agree that the gift of the breath of life comes from God, is it a legitimate thought, that the lungs, the organs which facilitate this breath, could be taken as the physical location of the contact between God's gift of life and man? If so, could it be, that Anne-Marie's heart was constructed in such a way that its main energy would be spent in bringing her lifeblood towards her lungs, this physical contact-location? Maybe she simply could not live with her heart's main energy re-channelled towards herself, and maybe, as an after-thought, to attempt such an operation was necessarily going to be unsuccessful. ...Just a thought to ponder.

21. The Orthodox Church of Saint John of Shanghai is at the corner of the Antrim Road and Cliftonville Road, Belfast. The link to it is: http://stjohnofshanghaibelfast.org/ You can see the icon on the front cover of the book in this church and you will be very welcome.

Love and God bless!

Johanna

About the Author

Johanna McBride, a mother of five, was born in Hamburg, Germany in 1960 as the second of two daughters of a Protestant family. She was given the name "Astrid". At the age of 19 she moved to England and studied philosophy and then occupational therapy and became an Occupational Therapist (OT) in 1986

She moved to Northern Ireland aged 28 and worked as an OT while actively exploring faith matters in the face of the deep divisions between the churches there. She regularly attended BOTH Catholic AND Protestant services.

In 1988 she had an experience of Salvation and of being set free to a new life of faith. From then onwards much of her life was spent in search of purity of faith, of love and of life. She was a voluntary worker living with handicapped adults in a Northern Irish Camphill Community for six months (www.camphill.org.uk), before becoming a voluntary live-in helper in the "Christian Renewal Centre" Rostrevor (www.crc-rostrevor.org) working for reconciliation among Christians in Northern Ireland

In 1990 she was married to Pat McBride, a devout Catholic. They have five children. Anne-Marie is/was their fourth child. They are now living in Belfast, Northern Ireland.

Astrid became a Catechumen of the Orthodox Church in December 2000 taking on the name "Johanna", and joined as a full member in January 2003. She is a committed member both of the Lamb of God Community[4] and of the Orthodox Church[21] and as a project during a course of study in Orthodox theology she produced the beautifully illustrated book: "Prepare ye the way of the Lord" in honour of St John the Baptist and Forerunner, also available from Lulu: http://www.lulu.com/shop/johanna-mcbride/prepare-ye-the-way-of-the-lord/paperback/product-5251073.html

Sue Fownes wrote…. (email 19th Sep. 2007)

…just to wish you luck with the manuscript.. I have started reading it…

I am only a quarter of the way…it is the most profound statement of love of a mother for her child, her children and her husband that I have ever read.

It moves me to tears and through your love of Christ you teach the spiritual truths. I have never read the Bible, but you have brought me closer. Thank God for your good friend that has supported you all these years to continue and to write what has and is in your mind and heart.

I have never read anything so clear and so beautiful in its simplicity…